Developing Numeracy
NUMBERS AND THE NUMBER SYSTEM
ACTIVITIES FOR THE DAILY MATHS LESSON

D1784145

year

3

Hilary Koll and Steve Mills

A & C BLACK

Contents

Estimating and rounding

Fractions

Reprinted 2000, 2001, 2002 (twice), 2004, 2005
Published 2000 by A&C Black Publishers Limited
37 Soho Square, London W1D 3QZ
www.acblack.com

ISBN O-7136-5234-9

Copyright text © Hilary Koll and Steve Mills, 2000
Copyright illustrations © Michael Evans, 2000
Copyright cover illustration © Charlotte Hard, 2000

The authors and publishers would like to thank the following teachers for their advice in producing this series of books:
Tracy Adam; Shilpa Bharambe; Hardip Channa; Sue Hall; Ann Hart; Lydia Hunt; Madeleine Madden; Helen Mason;
Anne Norbury; Jane Siddons; Judith Wells; Fleur Whatley.

A & C Black uses paper produced with elemental chlorine-free pulp, harvested from managed sustainable forests.
Printed in Great Britain by St Edmundsbury Press Ltd, Bury St Edmunds, Suffolk.

Introduction

Developing Numeracy: Numbers and the Number System is a series of seven photocopiable activity books designed to be used during the daily maths lesson. They focus on the first strand of the National Numeracy Strategy *Framework for teaching mathematics*. The activities are intended to be used in the time allocated to pupil activities; they aim to reinforce the teaching within the lesson and provide practice and consolidation of the objectives contained within the framework document.

Year 3 supports the teaching of mathematics to Year 3 children by providing a series of activities to develop essential skills in counting; recognising properties of numbers and number sequences; place value and ordering; estimating and rounding; and understanding fractions. On the whole they are designed for children to undertake independently during the period of the daily maths lesson which is allocated to pupil activities.

Year 3:

- develops an understanding of the relationships between numbers through estimating, ordering, counting on or back and exploring place value;
- examines properties of numbers and number sequences;
- includes activities which focus on recognising and using fractions;
- promotes independent work during the daily maths lesson with low guidance activities;
- encourages the use of correct mathematical language.

Extension

Many of the activity sheets end with a challenge (**Now try this!**) which reinforces and extends the children's learning, and provides the teacher with the opportunity for assessment. Where children are asked to carry out an activity, the instructions are clear to enable them to work independently, although the teacher may wish to read out the instructions and provide further support where necessary. The children may need to write their answers on a separate piece of paper.

Organisation

The activities do not require many additional resources, but coloured pencils, cubes, counters, scissors, number lines, place value cards (also called arrow cards) and a 100-square may be useful. Several of the sheets involve cutting out cards, which can be done by the children themselves, or by an adult beforehand. To help teachers to select appropriate learning experiences for their children, the activities are grouped into sections within each book. The pages are not intended to be presented in the order in which they appear unless otherwise stated.

Teachers' notes

Very brief notes are provided at the end of most pages, giving ideas and suggestions for maximising the effectiveness of the activity sheets. These notes could be masked before photocopying.

Structure of the daily maths lesson

The recommended structure of the daily maths lesson for Key Stage 2 is as follows:

Start to lesson, oral work, mental calculation	5-10 minutes
Main teaching and pupil activities	about 40 minutes
Plenary	about 10 minutes

Each lesson should include:
- a focused start with the whole class involved in oral and mental counting work;
- some direct interactive teaching of the whole class on the maths objective for the day;
- group or individual activities linked to the objective of the lesson. The teacher should focus on one group to continue teaching directly. The activities in the **Developing Numeracy** books are designed to be carried out in the time allocated to pupil activities;
- a plenary with the whole class when the pupil activities are ended to consolidate and extend the children's learning through questions and discussion.

The following chart shows an example of the way in which an activity from this book can be used to achieve the required organisation of the daily maths lesson for Year 3 children.

Follow the paths (page 33)

Start to the lesson	
Begin by seating the children in a circle and asking them to count around the circle in ones, starting from any number. When you clap your hands the children should begin to count backwards from the number they have reached, for example, 343, 344, 345, 346 (clap), 345, 344, 343, 342 and so on. Repeat this activity for counting on and back in tens and hundreds from two- or three-digit numbers.	**5-10 minutes**

Main teaching and pupil activities	
Write a three-digit number on the board and ask children to say how many ones, tens and hundreds it has. Use place value (arrow) cards to demonstrate and partition the number in the following way: 345 = 300 + 40 + 5. Ask children to say which number is one more than this number (346). Do the tens or hundreds digits change? Demonstrate how to find one more or less than a range of three-digit numbers, including numbers with 9 or 0, for example: 239 + 1 or 540 – 1. Now demonstrate how to find ten or one hundred more or less than a number, using place value cards to show how the number changes. Afterwards, the children could work on **Follow the paths** (page 33, **Developing Numeracy: Numbers and the Number System Year 3**).	**about 40 minutes**

Plenary	
Discuss the children's answers and go over a few examples on the board. Draw attention to those questions which involve crossing a tens or hundreds boundary, for example: 49 + 1. Invite the children to explain how they worked out the answers and demonstrate these on a number line.	**about 10 minutes**

Further activities

These activities provide some practical ideas for whole class mental and oral work. They are intended to introduce or reinforce the main teaching part of the lesson.

Counting, properties of numbers and number sequences

Counting stick
You will need a stick which is divided into ten equal coloured sections (such as a metre stick with each 10 cm coloured). Hold the stick so that all the children can see it and point to each section along it in turn. Decide on a number (for example, four) and ask children to count in fours as you point to each section. This provides practice in counting forwards and backwards and helps the children to remember the multiples of the given number.

Show me
Each child has two sets of digit cards from 0 to 9. Play 'show me' activities, where each child shows a number by holding one or two digit cards in the air. Give instructions such as, *"Show me an even number between 31 and 39... a multiple of two... the highest odd number you can make with two cards."*

Jumping along
Ask the children to count on or back from a given starting number, for example: *"Count backwards in ones from 57. Count forward in tens from 43."* This can be played in groups or around the whole class.

Adding ones and tens
Using a large 100-square, place a piece of plasticine on the number 1. Ask a child to choose one of two cards you are holding which show +1 or +10. The child then places a new piece of plasticine on the corresponding number (2 or 11). Continue the activity, creating a trail through the 100-square, until no more movement is possible.

Place value and ordering

Show me place value
Give each child a set of place value cards. These may also be called arrow cards (see **Developing Numeracy: Numbers and the Number System Year 2** for a photocopiable set). Play 'show me' activities where each child shows a number by holding one or two digit cards in the air, for example: *"Show me number 63. How many tens and how many ones? Show me the number between 69 and 71."*

People numbers
Invite ten children to stand at the front of the class. Give each child a card with a two or three-digit number on it, which they hold in front of them, facing the rest of the class. Ask the children to arrange themselves in order, from highest to lowest. Then invite individual children who are not holding a number to change places with those at the front. (*"Jo, change places with 167; Irfan, change places with any multiple of ten."*)

Totals
Draw a 'dartboard' like the one shown here. Ask the children to imagine they have three darts and challenge the children with questions such as: *"Can you score 19... 83... 310... 40? How many different scores between 100 and 150 can you make? What is the highest score you can make? What is the lowest? Which is the nearest score to 125?"*

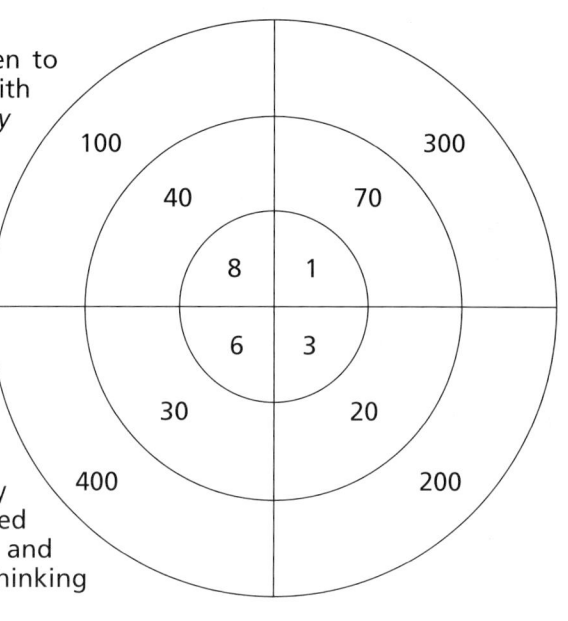

Estimating and rounding

Numbers in the environment
Encourage the children to estimate the numbers of objects in and around the classroom (for example, the number of children in the school, chairs in the classroom, cubes in a tray). Discuss with the children examples of numbers they can see and hear around them which exemplify the number work they are doing. Car registration numbers and bus numbers can be used for place value, door numbers for simple number sequences and half and quarter past the hour can provide an opportunity for thinking about fractions in a real context.

Fractions

Fraction groups
Invite four children to the front and ask the class to answer questions about the group, for example: *"What fraction of these children are girls/boys? What fraction have brown hair/blue eyes? What fraction of them have black shoes/white socks?"* As the children become more confident with fractions of sets, the number of children can vary. Invite ten children to the front and explore the equivalence of fractions, explaining for example, *"If five tenths of the children are boys, half of the children are boys"*.

Fractions on a number line
Ask the children to count on or back along sections of a number line in steps of fractions (for example, one half or one quarter). As the children are chanting, encourage them to shout the whole numbers to develop a rhythm, for example: *"two and a half, **three**, three and a half, **four**"*.

Selected answers

p 7
24
41
26 34
43

p 8
21
35
24

p 20
Multiples of two:
18, 22, 46, 48

Multiples of five:
15, 35, 45, 205
Multiples of two and five:
10, 160, 200
Multiples of neither:
17, 63, 13

p 34
Red: 175, 184, 274, 173, 164, 74
Orange: 905, 914, 1004, 903, 894, 804
Blue: 864, 873, 963, 862, 853, 763

Green: 296, 305, 395, 294, 285, 195
Yellow: 520, 529, 619, 518, 509, 419
Purple: 798, 807, 897, 796, 787, 697

Now try this!
179, 188, 278, 177, 168, 78

p 39
21 30
57 94

p 51
3 2
2 3
4 2
5 4

p 53
1. 12   2. 8
3. 9   4. 8
5. 12   6. 12
7. 9   8. 4

Sorting sweets

- **Sort the sweets into sets of** ten.
- **Circle each set of ten.**
- **Write the total number of sweets in the box.**

Count carefully.
There may be
sweets left over.

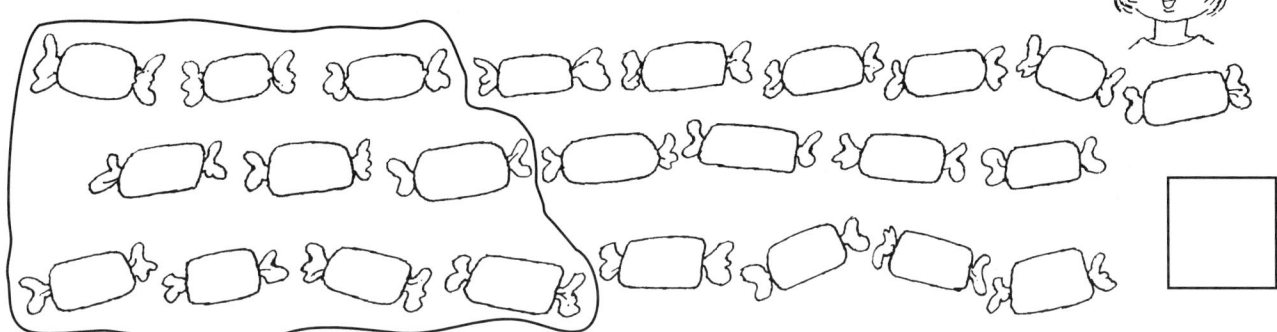

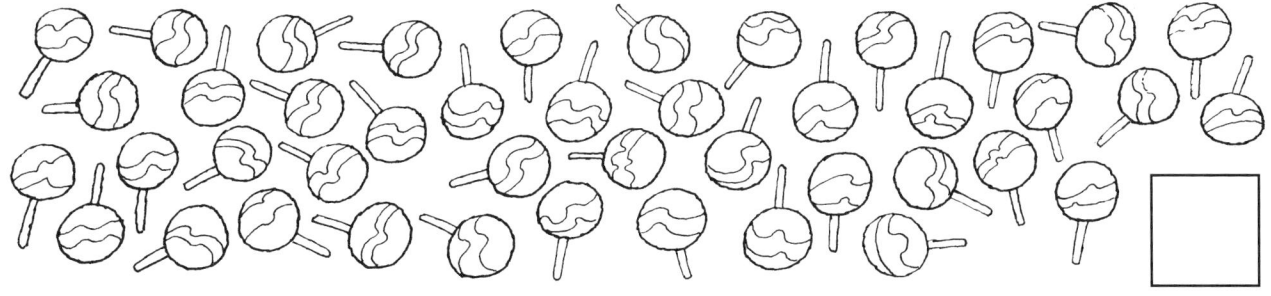

- **Draw some sweets of your own.**
- **Ask a friend to sort them into groups of ten.**

Now try this!

Teachers' note Remind the children to count carefully, and suggest that they check each group of ten. As an additional extension activity, ask the children to find the total number in a set of cubes. Suggest that they join the cubes together in groups of ten to help them count. Make sure the children are familiar with both of the terms 'set' and 'group'.

Developing Numeracy
Numbers and the Number System
Year 3
© A & C Black

All sorts of sorting

- **Sort the toys into sets.**
- **Write the total number in the box.**

Count carefully. There may be toys left over.

Sort the cars and lorries into sets of ⌊five⌋.

Sort the marbles into sets of ⌊three⌋.

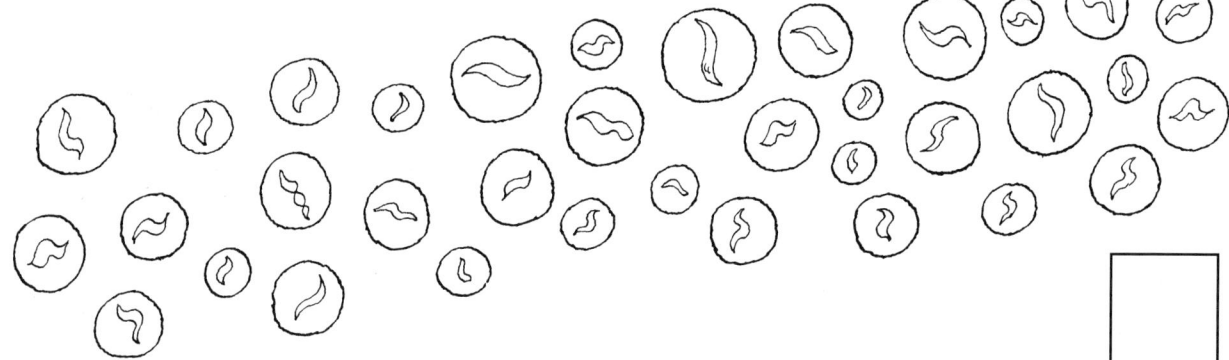

Sort the yo-yos into sets of ⌊six⌋.

Now try this!

- **Count 26 cubes.**
- **Sort them into groups of three cubes, then four cubes, then five cubes, then six cubes.**
- **Write how many groups you make each time.**

Teachers' note To consolidate the children's understanding, maximise opportunities for sorting the class into groups of different sizes. For example, in PE lessons, arrange the children into six groups of four with one left over, or four groups of six with one left over, or four groups of five. Make sure the children are familiar with both of the terms 'set' and 'group'.

Developing Numeracy
Numbers and the Number System
Year 3
© A & C Black

Number snakes

- **Write the missing numbers on the snakes.**

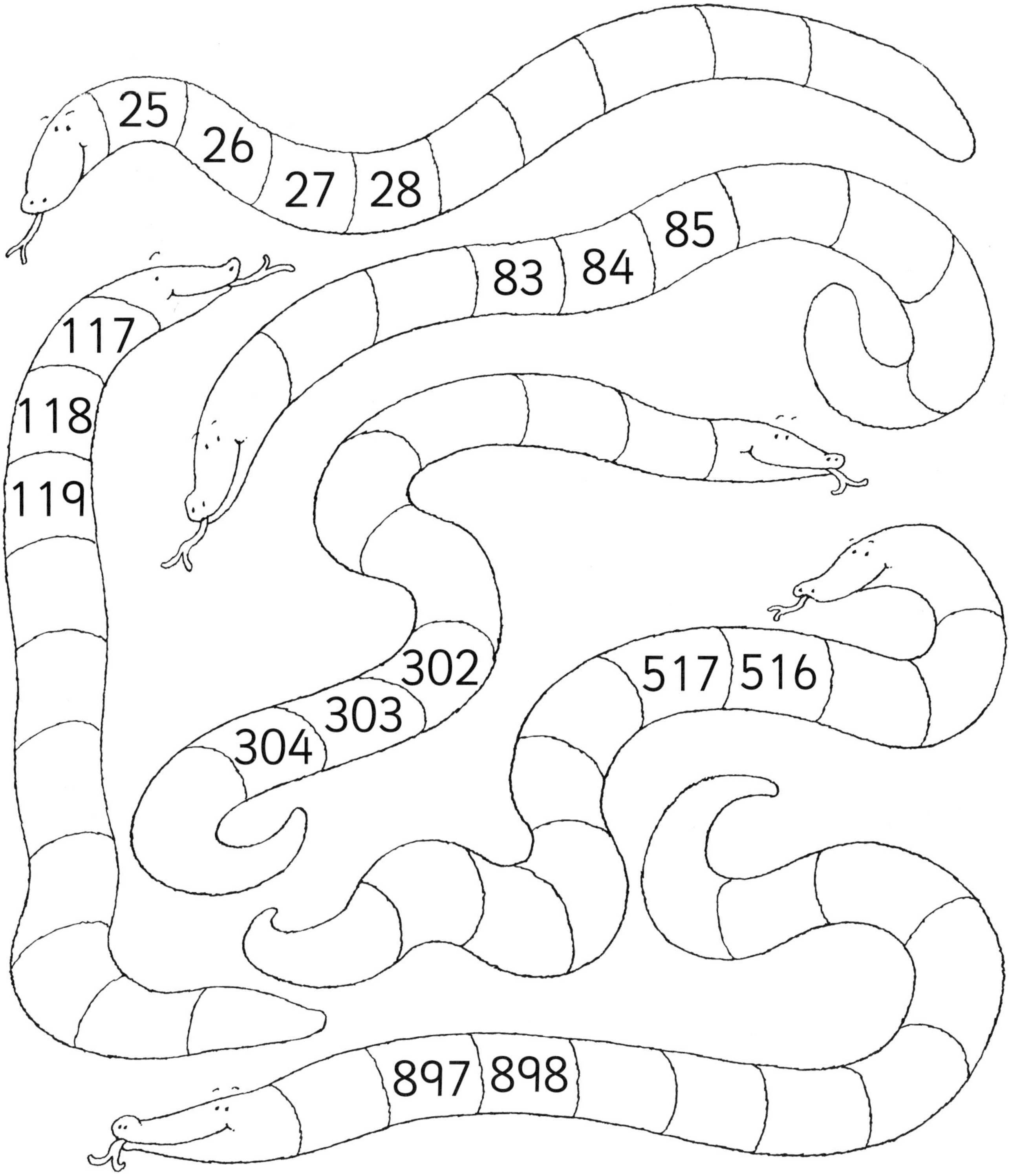

25 26 27 28

83 84 85

117
118
119

302 303 304

517 516

897 898

- **Make three more number snakes for a friend to complete.**

Teachers' note Encourage the children to read the numbers in the snakes aloud once they have completed them. This gives the children practice in reading larger numbers and can help them to check and remember number sequences.

Developing Numeracy
Numbers and the Number System
Year 3
© A & C Black

Sliding backwards

- **Count back in** ones **down each ladder.**

18
17
16

22

61

101

423

274

200

110

555

- **Make five more number ladders for a friend to complete.**
- **Try starting on a number above 500.**

Now try this!

Teachers' note Encourage the children to read the numbers in the completed ladders aloud. The numbers on this sheet can be masked before photocopying for a more flexible resource.

Developing Numeracy
Numbers and the Number System
Year 3
© A & C Black

Stepping stones

• **Count on or back in** ⌐tens⌐ **each time to cross the river.**

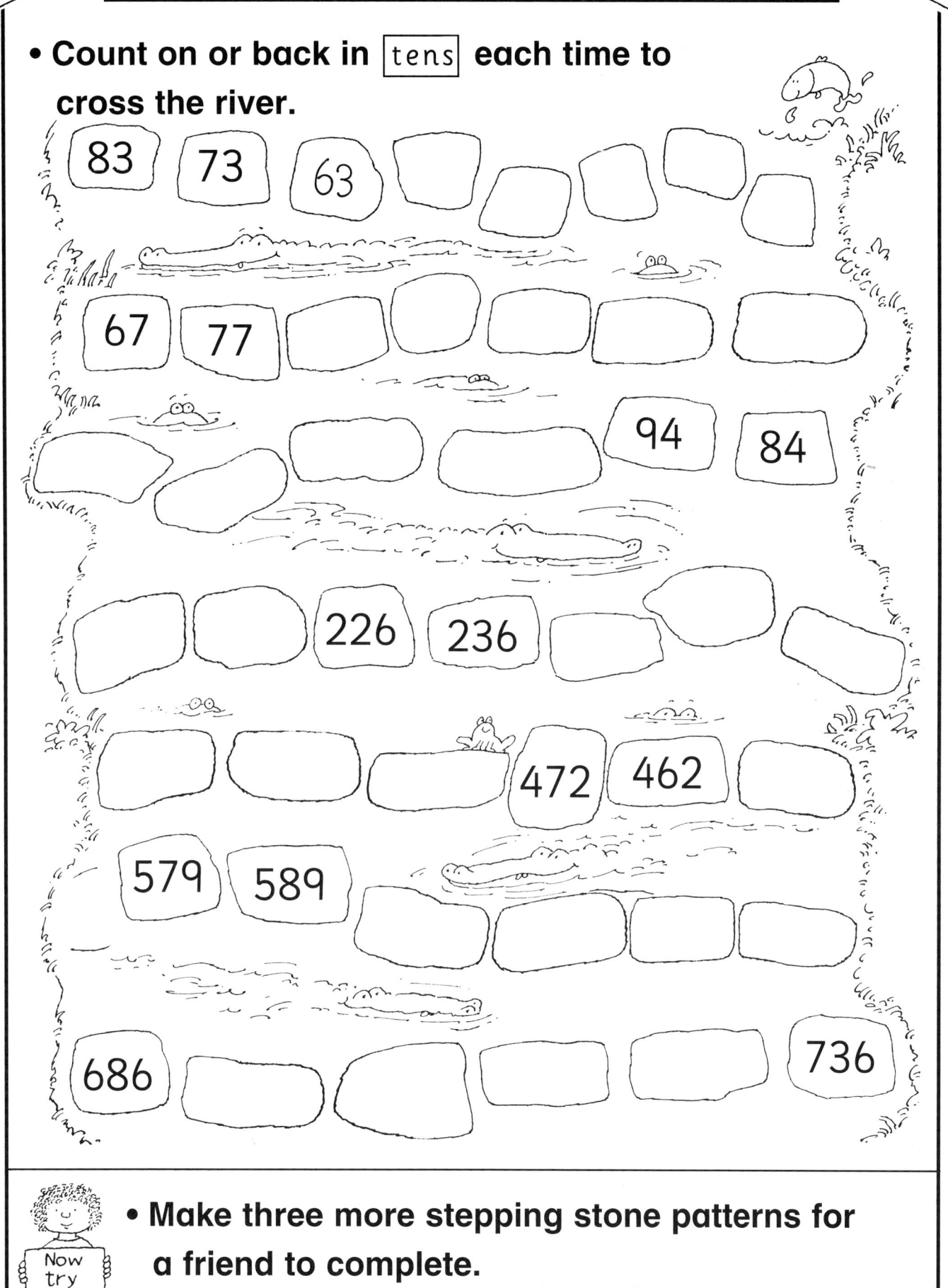

83　73　63

67　77

94　84

226　236

472　462

579　589

686　　　　　　　736

• **Make three more stepping stone patterns for a friend to complete.**

Now try this!

Teachers' note To introduce the activity, show the children some of the number patterns made from place value cards, emphasising how the tens digit changes each time.

Developing Numeracy
Numbers and the Number System
Year 3
© A & C Black

Animals in order

- **Write the numbers on the animals in order.**
Start with the largest number.

83 73

33   63   43   7̶3̶   23   53   8̶3̶

114   144   94   164   124   154   104   174   134

189   199   269   219   259   209   249   229   239

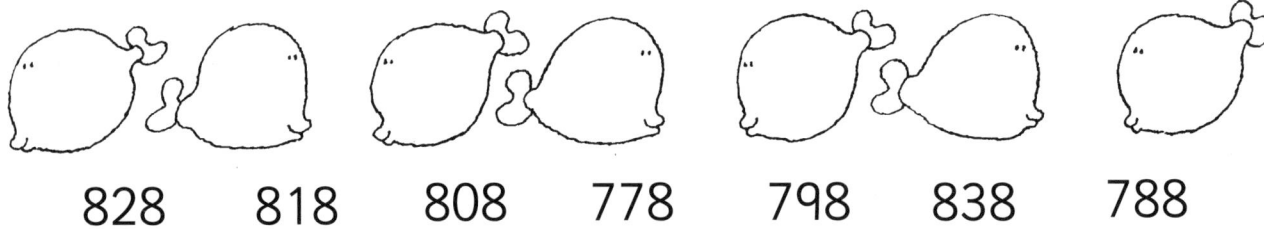

828   818   808   778   798   838   788

- **Work out which numbers are missing.**
- **Write all the numbers in order.**

Now try this!

929

939   ?   989   ?   9̶2̶9̶   959   ?

Teachers' note The numbers on this sheet can be masked before photocopying for a more flexible resource.

**Developing Numeracy
Numbers and the Number System
Year 3
© A & C Black**

One hundred more

- **Start with the shaded number. Colour the numbers that are exactly** 100 more **each time.**

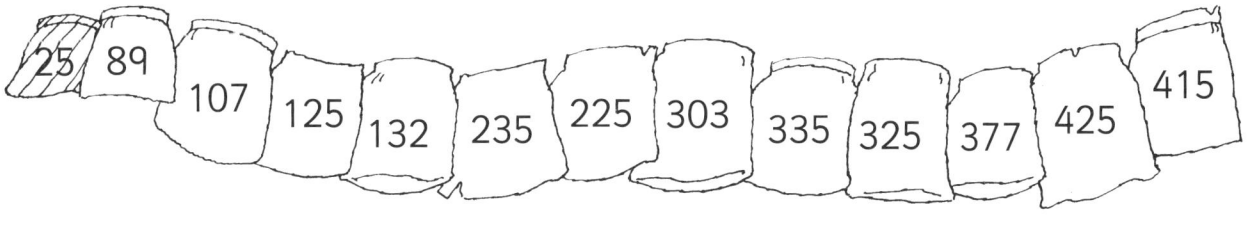

25 89 107 125 132 235 225 303 335 325 377 425 415

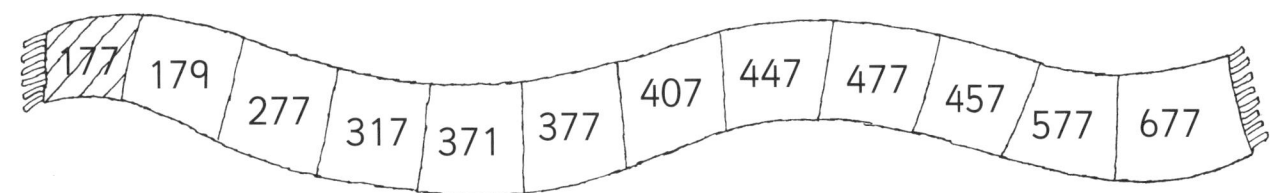

177 179 277 317 371 377 407 447 477 457 577 677

269 279 349 369 469 50 569 669 709 769

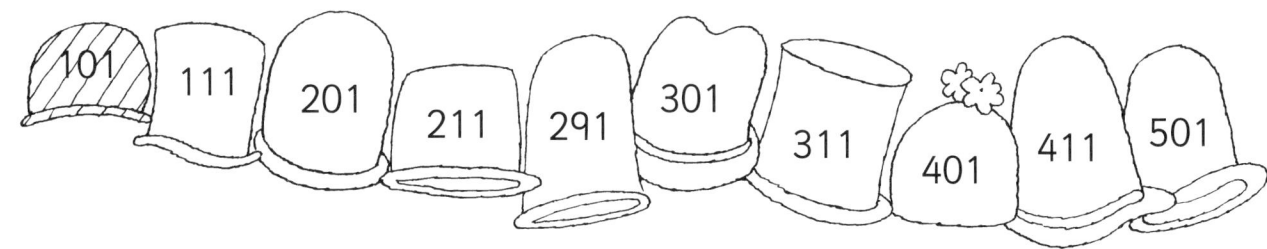

101 111 201 211 291 301 311 401 411 501

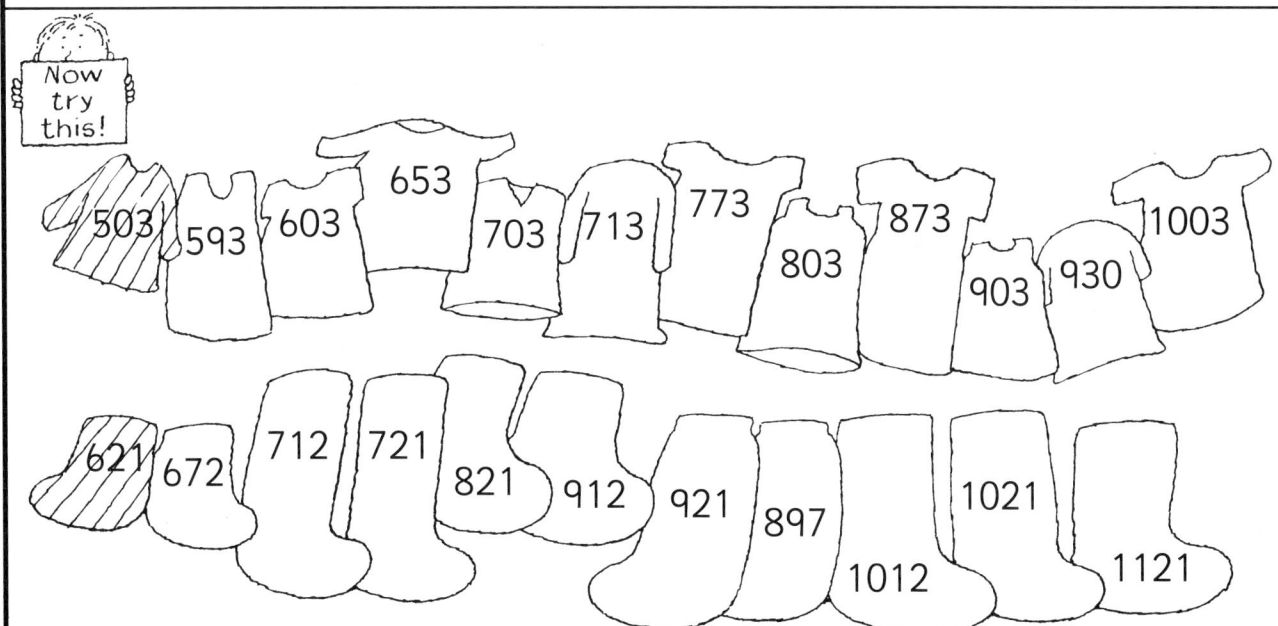

Now try this!

503 593 603 653 703 713 773 873 803 903 930 1003

621 672 712 721 821 912 921 897 1012 1021 1121

Teachers' note As an introductory or extension activity, the children could play the following game: one child says a three-digit number, then each child in the group takes it in turns to add on 100 and say the number aloud.

Developing Numeracy
Numbers and the Number System
Year 3
© A & C Black

13

One hundred less

• **Write the missing numbers on the clothes.**

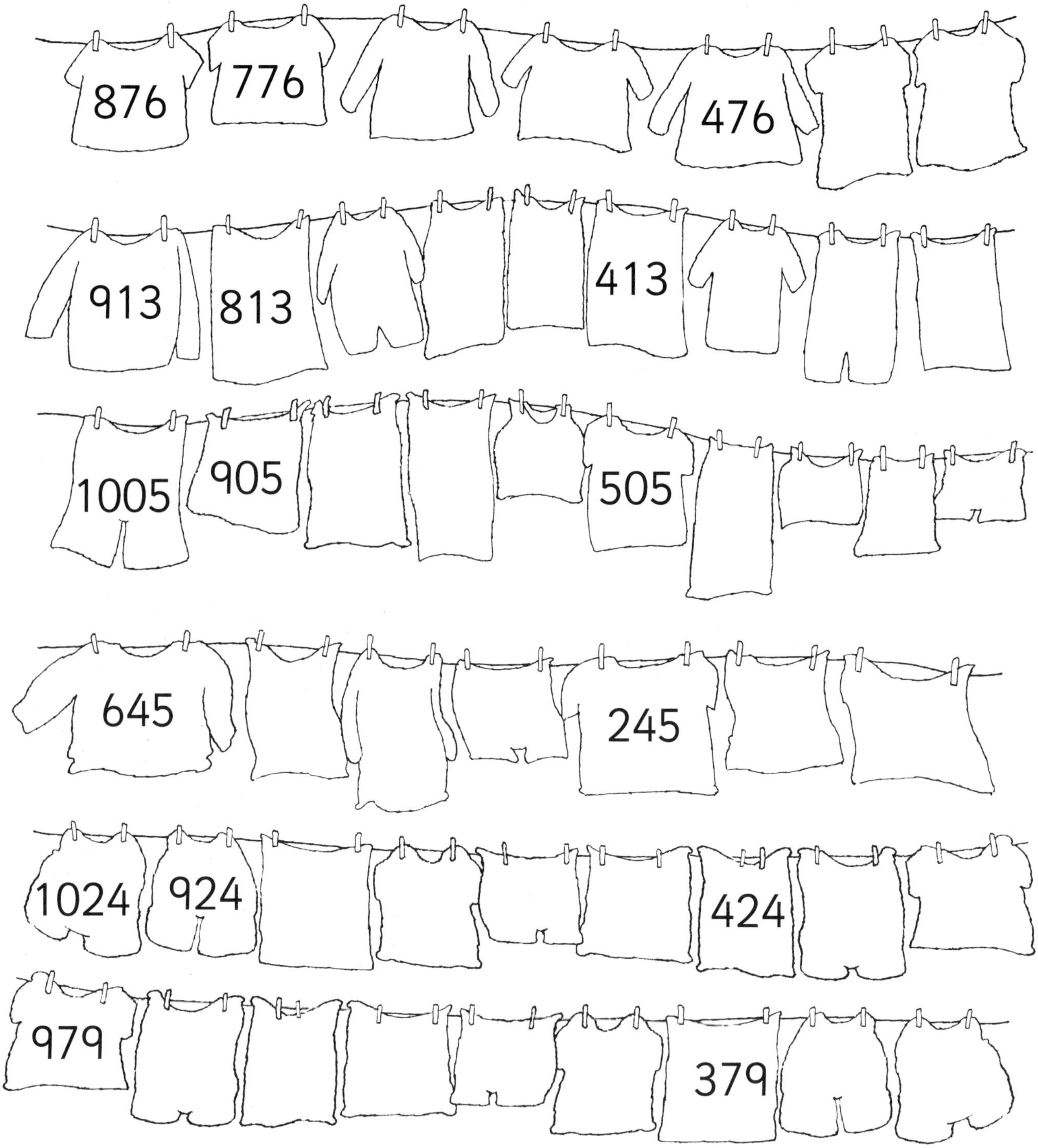

876   776   ⬚   ⬚   476   ⬚   ⬚

913   813   ⬚   413   ⬚   ⬚   ⬚

1005   905   ⬚   ⬚   505   ⬚   ⬚   ⬚

645   ⬚   ⬚   ⬚   245   ⬚   ⬚

1024   924   ⬚   ⬚   ⬚   424   ⬚

979   ⬚   ⬚   ⬚   ⬚   379   ⬚

Now try this!

• **Draw three more number washing lines for a friend to complete.**
• **Start with a number above 1000.**

Teachers' note Use place value cards to demonstrate these number patterns to the children. Emphasise how the hundreds digit changes each time.

Developing Numeracy
Numbers and the Number System
Year 3
© A & C Black

Cross the bridge

Find your way across the bridges.

- Step on the numbers that are two more or two less than the last number you stepped on.

- Shade each step you take.

The first one goes back in twos.

79 77 76 75 73 72 71 69 68 67 66 65 63 61
start

18 19 20 21 22 23 24 25 26 27 28 29 30 31 32 33 34
start

86 84 83 82 80 79 78 77 76 74 73 72 71 70 68
start

53 55 56 57 58 59 60 61 63 65 66 67 68 69 70 71 73 75
start

Look carefully. The last one goes on <u>and</u> back in twos.

35 36 37 35 34 37 38 39 41 43 42 41 39 37 38 35 37
start

- Draw two more number bridges for a friend to walk across.

Now try this!

They could go on and back in twos.

Teachers' note The children could use a 100-square to help them to work independently on this activity. As an additional activity, the following game can be played as a group or whole class: one child says a number between one and ten, the next child adds on two, and so on until you say 'stop'. The children then subtract two from each number.

**Developing Numeracy
Numbers and the Number System
Year 3**
© A & C Black

15

Odd or even?

- **Colour all the** odd numbers **to find the path through the grid.**

 Look at the units digit to help you.

start

94	1	70	502	186	52	14	102	406	97	241	801
210	407	614	220	320	120	70	6	508	601	152	687
236	57	128	510	92	174	520	250	183	309	242	53
95	249	82	410	240	126	326	110	611	518	400	21
19	24	608	62	72	212	246	4	71	216	190	323
327	181	153	102	304	506	174	74	415	79	88	55
4	124	613	84	516	80	328	101	93	107	122	339
308	322	5	414	606	187	103	17	104	64	406	133
661	51	243	76	34	113	500	78	308	512	8	75
403	504	214	328	619	105	244	86	606	416	111	163
99	10	418	44	73	92	104	130	58	610	7	246
123	13	169	519	241	218	322	144	322	244	189	772

finish

 Now try this!

- **Write a rule to show how to work out if a number is odd or even.**

Teachers' note If the grid is coloured correctly, there will be a trail from the start to the finishing box, passing through odd numbers only. As an additional whole-class activity, play 'show me' with digit cards. Ask the children to show you numbers such as 'an even number between 21 and 41'.

Developing Numeracy
Numbers and the Number System
Year 3
© A & C Black

16

Number lorries

- Write four even numbers between 20 and 40.

- Write four odd numbers between 40 and 60.

- Write **all** the even numbers between 37 and 57 in this lorry.

- Write **all** the odd numbers between 18 and 38 in this lorry.

- Write **all** the odd numbers between 10 and 100 that have two digits the same.

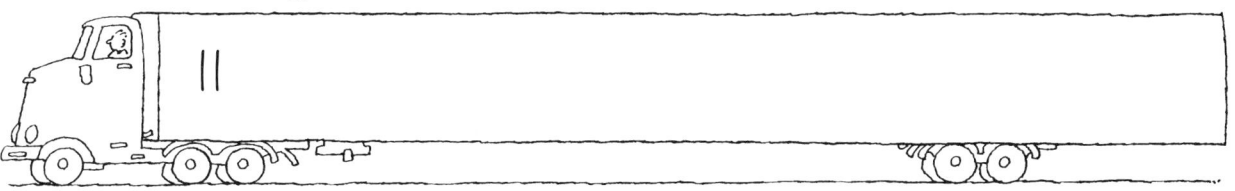

11

- Write **all** the even numbers between 100 and 1000 that have three digits the same.

Now try this!

222

Teachers' note Make sure that the children read each instruction carefully and encourage them to describe how they can be sure if a number is odd or even. Ask the children to investigate rules for adding two even numbers together and two odd numbers together.

Developing Numeracy
Numbers and the Number System
Year 3
© A & C Black

Climbing mountains

• Write the correct number on each step.

count up

count down

27
24
21

count in threes

0 3 6

count in fours

4 8 12

count in fives

6 11 16

count in threes

7 10 13

count in fours

1 5 9

Now try this!

77

count down in sevens

count up in sixes

Teachers' note For the main activity, the children should check their answers to see if the ascending and descending numbers are the same.

Developing Numeracy
Numbers and the Number System
Year 3
© A & C Black

18

Going up! Coming down!

• **Complete the patterns in the lifts.**

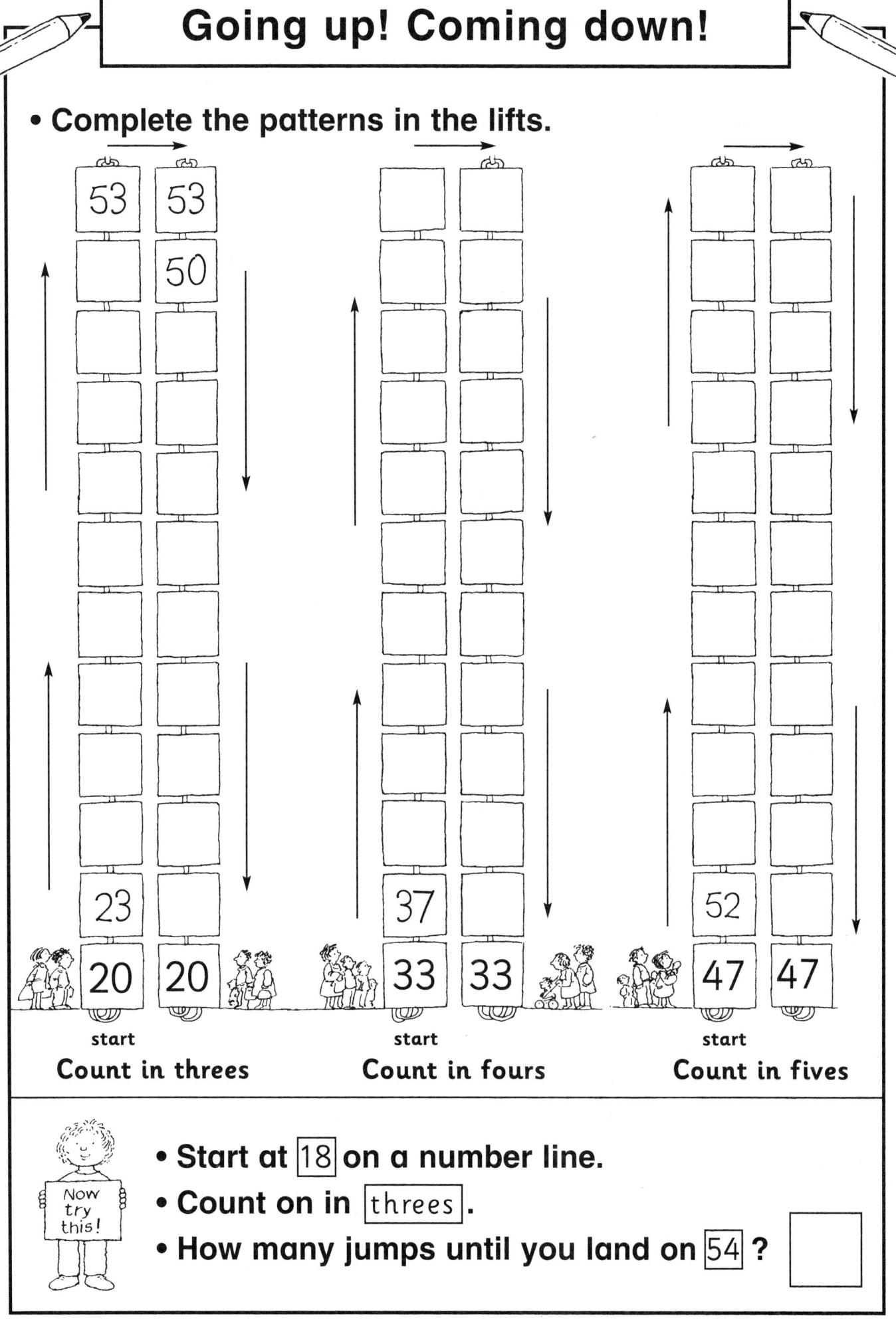

Count in threes

Count in fours

Count in fives

• **Start at** 18 **on a number line.**

• **Count on in** threes .

• **How many jumps until you land on** 54 **?**

Teachers' note Provide 0-100 number lines and a counter for those children who may need help to complete this activity.

Developing Numeracy
Numbers and the Number System
Year 3
© A & C Black

Can you sort it?

- **Look at the numbers in the box.**
- **Write them in the correct place on the Venn diagram.**

Some numbers are multiples of two <u>and</u> five.

22	15	46	18	10	17	35
48	200	160	45	63	13	205

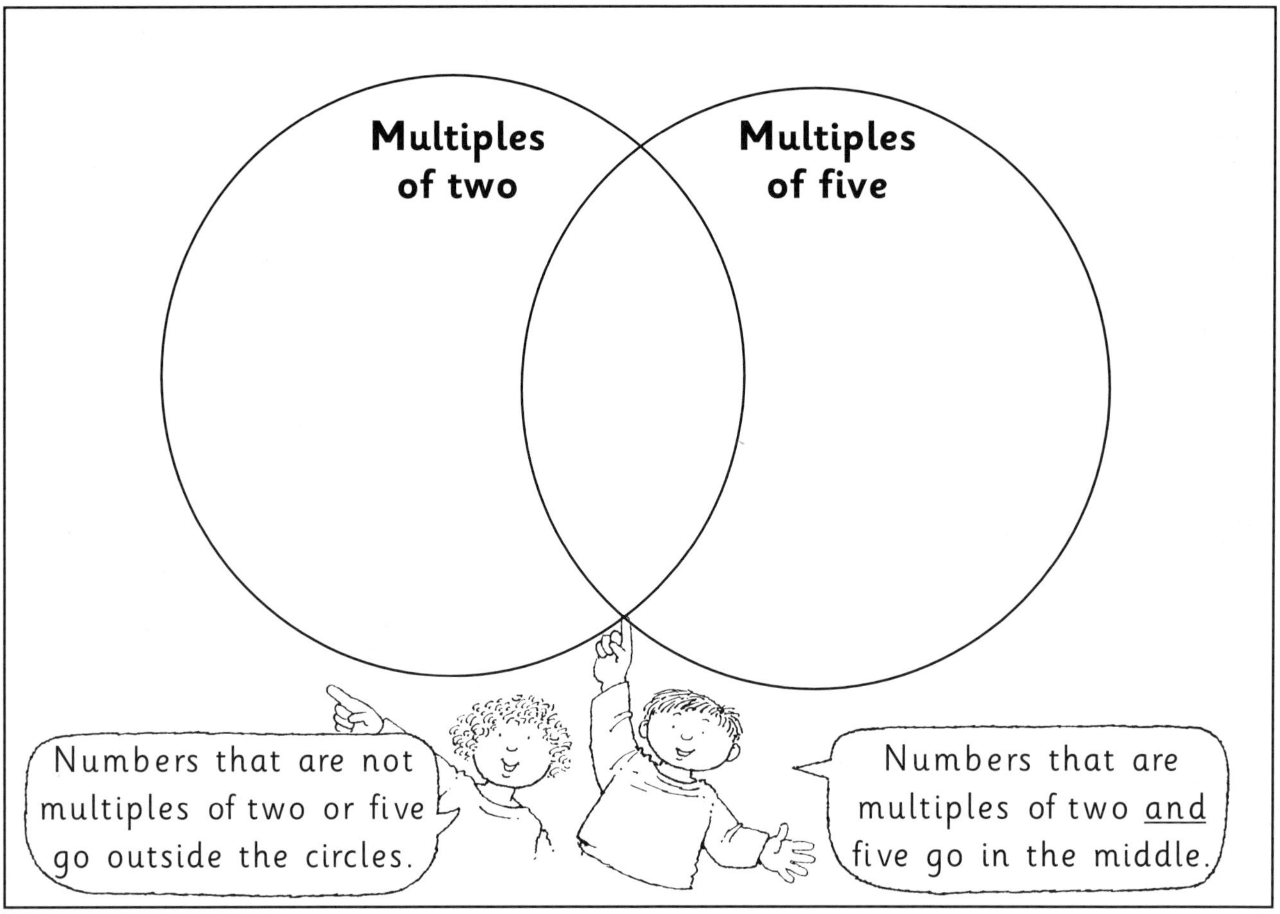

Multiples of two   **Multiples of five**

Numbers that are not multiples of two or five go outside the circles.

Numbers that are multiples of two <u>and</u> five go in the middle.

Now try this!

- **Which numbers on the Venn diagram are** multiples of ten **?** _____

- **Write all the** multiples of ten **between 151 and 205.** _____

- **Which of these numbers are also** multiples of two and five **?** _____

Teachers' note Use hoops and number cards to introduce the children to Venn diagrams of this type. Demonstrate how numbers can be in two hoops at the same time.

Developing Numeracy
Numbers and the Number System
Year 3
© A & C Black

Multiple mix-up

The multiples are in a mess!

- Sort the numbers and write them in the correct boxes.

Some numbers belong in more than one box.

200

Multiples of 100

200

Multiples of 50

250

170

700

410

400

200

200

800   900

Multiples of 10

350   680

600

260   450

540

130   510

- Write a rule to say how you can recognise a |multiple of 10| and a |multiple of 50|.

Now try this!

Teachers' note Encourage the children to be systematic. They should look at each number in turn and work out which boxes it belongs to.

Developing Numeracy
Numbers and the Number System
Year 3
© A & C Black

21

Make it match

• **Match each pencil to the correct pencil sharpener.**

twelve	34
thirty-four	27
sixty	15
eighty-eight	36
fifteen	22
forty-seven	12
thirty-six	88
twenty-two	60
ninety-eight	53
twenty-seven	47
fifty-three	109
one hundred and nine	98

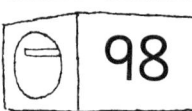

• **Write** in words **all the numbers from 59 to 71.**

Teachers' note Provide correct spellings of number words against which the children can check their answers.

Developing Numeracy
Numbers and the Number System
Year 3
© A & C Black

22

Road maze

- **Read the number word, then find the matching number on a road. Colour the road.**
- **Try the next one. Where do you end up?**

start

| Seven hundred and eighty-six |
| Nine hundred and four |
| One thousand, one hundred and seventeen |
| Nine hundred and twenty-six |
| Seven hundred and forty-three |
| Nine hundred and fifty-four |
| Four hundred and sixty-one |
| Six hundred and two |
| Five hundred and ninety-seven |
| Seven hundred and twelve |
| Six hundred and six |

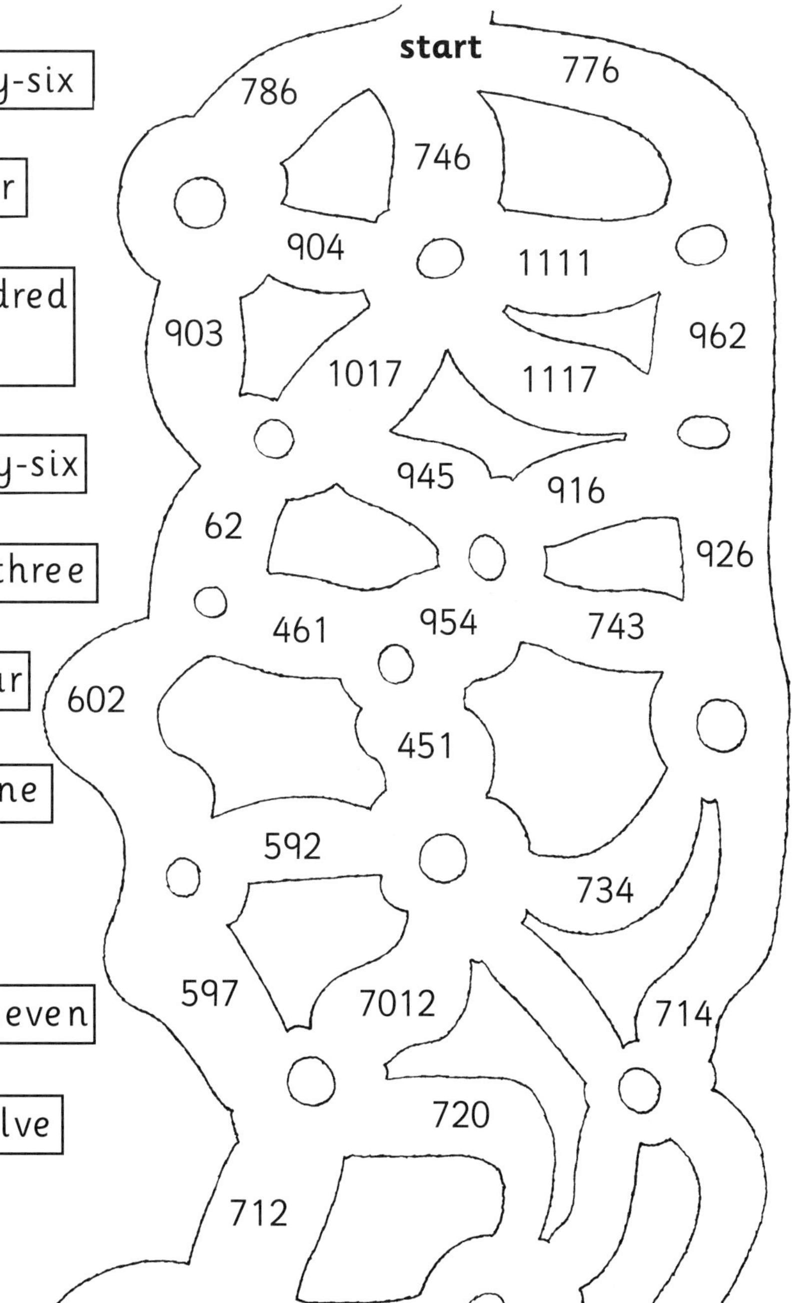

start

786 776 746 904 1111 903 962 1017 1117 945 916 62 926 461 954 743 602 451 592 734 597 7012 714 720 712 6006 66 616 6016 606 6106

hotel

theme park

farm

ice rink

bowling alley

Teachers' note As an extension activity, ask the children to write a list of the sequence of numbers (in words and figures) which would lead to another of the destinations on the map.

Developing Numeracy
Numbers and the Number System
Year 3
© A & C Black

Writing numbers

• **Write these numbers** in words .

 97 _____

 36 _____

104 _____

242 _____

680 _____

• **Write these numbers** in figures .

One hundred and twelve →

Seven hundred and forty-eight ←

Nine hundred and nine →

Eight hundred and thirteen ←

Six hundred and sixty →

 • **Write these numbers** in words .

 1793    8015    9301

Teachers' note The children could make their own set of cards to help them practise reading and recognising number names.

Developing Numeracy
Numbers and the Number System
Year 3
© A & C Black

Number search

- **Find each number in the grid.**
- **Draw a ring around it.**

The numbers may be vertical, horizontal or diagonal.

Nine hundred and nine

One hundred and eighty-one

Ninety-nine

Five hundred and fifty-six

Three hundred and twenty-nine

Seven hundred and sixty-three

Six hundred and three

Four hundred and seventy-five

Five hundred and thirty

Two hundred and twelve

One thousand and twenty

One thousand, one hundred and eleven

Three hundred and ninety-four

Eight hundred and forty-seven

Eight hundred and fifty-two

Three hundred and three

1	6	3	0	2	5	6	3	9	4	5	7	6	3
8	0	4	5	9	1	9	7	2	1	8	3	4	5
6	3	8	2	9	0	9	4	6	3	4	2	0	5
4	1	1	1	1	2	5	7	8	3	6	9	1	3
6	2	5	6	3	0	7	4	1	8	1	7	4	2
5	9	5	1	8	3	2	9	6	4	4	9	9	1
3	9	6	2	7	4	7	5	3	7	8	6	5	2
8	5	2	7	1	5	1	8	6	2	9	3	0	3

Now try this!

- **Find six four-digit numbers in the grid.**
- **Write the numbers in words.**

Teachers' note Before starting the extension activity, make sure that the children are familiar with the term 'four-digit numbers'.

Developing Numeracy
Numbers and the Number System
Year 3
© A & C Black

Tens and units game

- **Roll two dice to make a** two-digit number.
- **Put a counter on the abacus**
  that shows your number.
  Can you make four in a line?

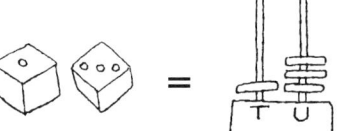

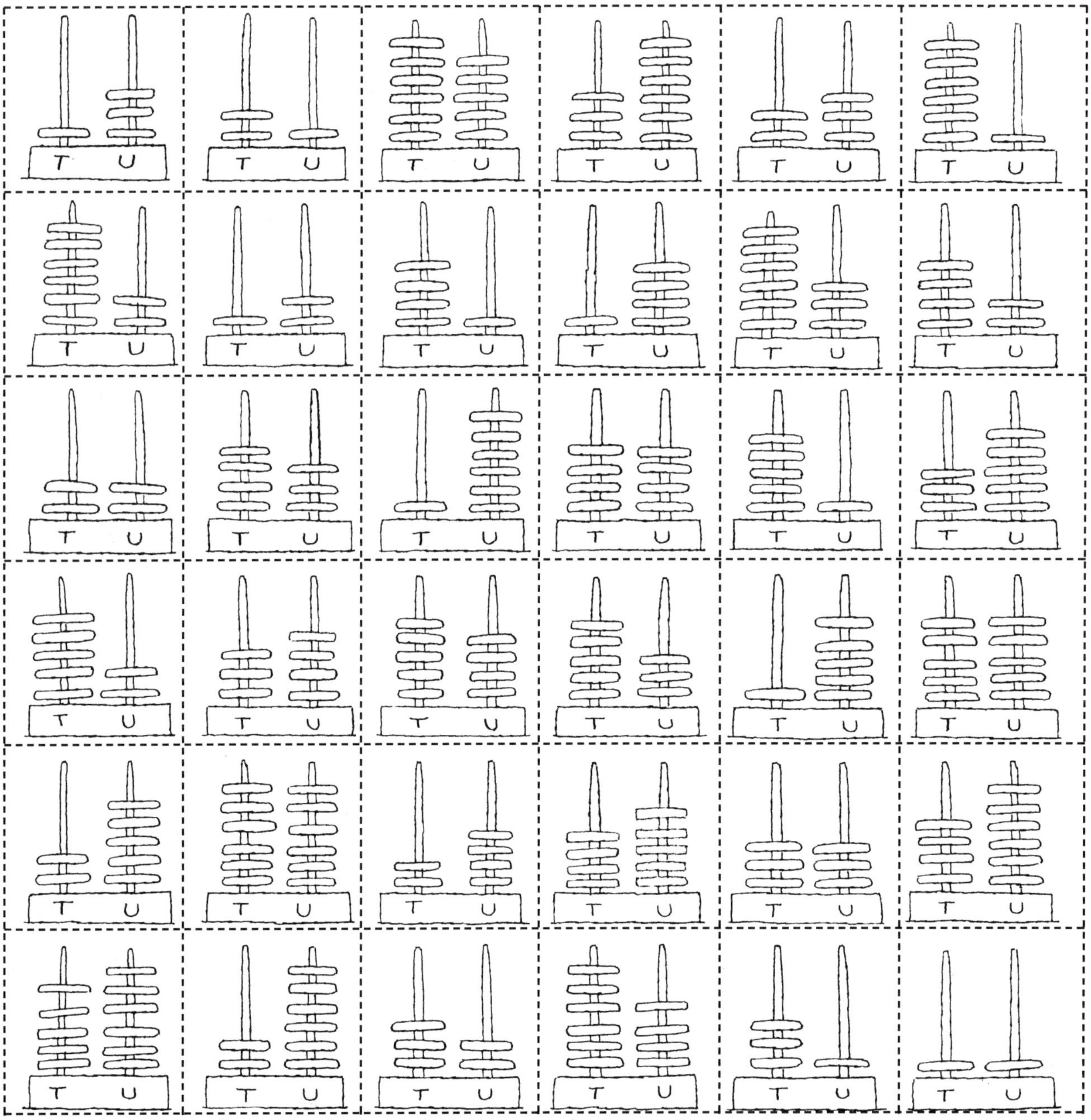

- **Cut out the cards and put them face down.**
- **Pick up four at a time and put them in order.**
  Start with the smallest.

Teachers' note This can be a game for two children. The winner is first to make four in a line in any direction. Remind the children that a tens and units number can also be called a two-digit number and encourage them to say the numbers aloud, as this helps them to relate the visual picture to the number. In the extension activity, the children could check one another's answers.

Developing Numeracy
Numbers and the Number System
Year 3
© A & C Black

Split the numbers

- **Split each number into tens and units.**

Example:  74 → 70 | 4

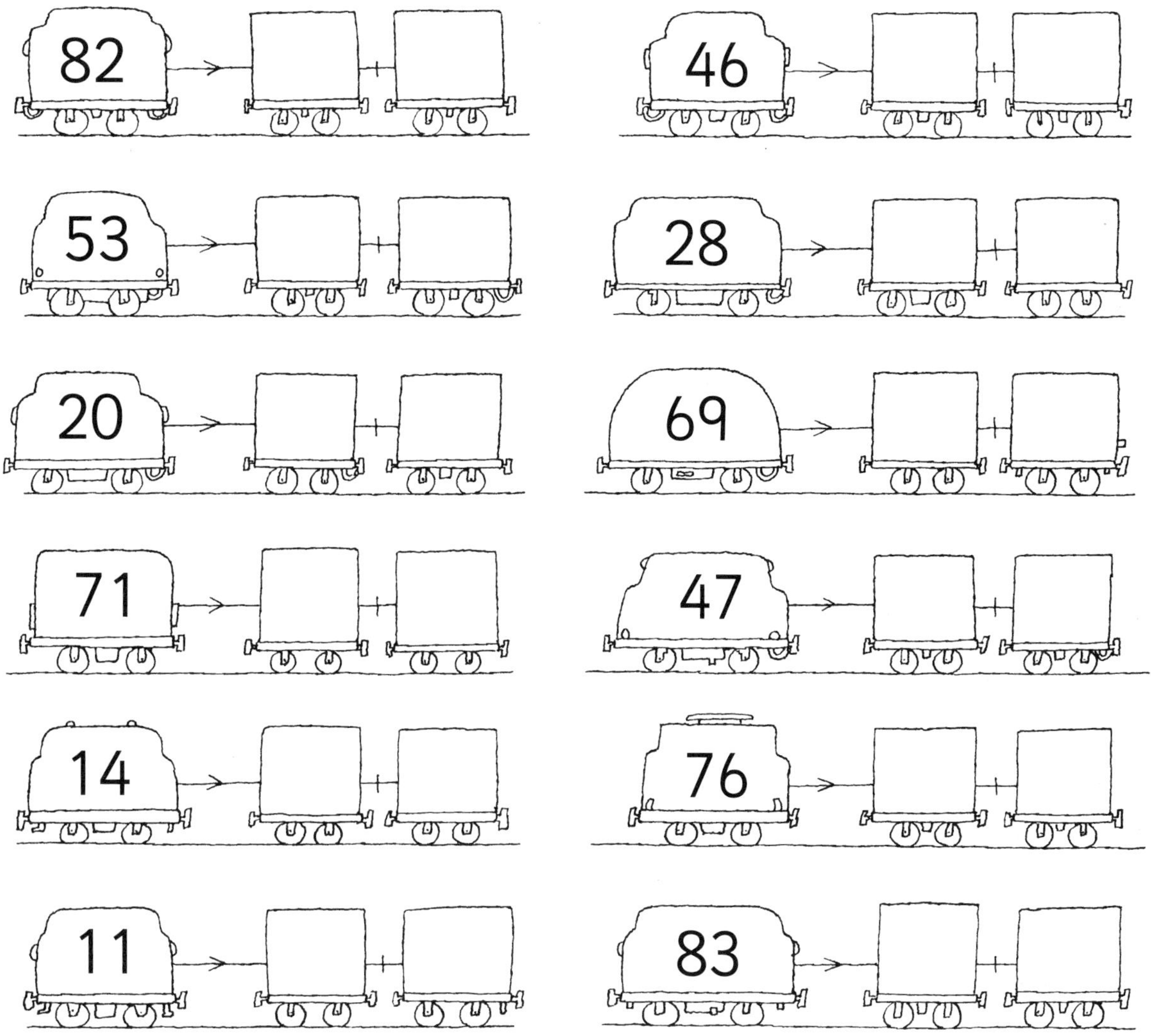

82 →

46 →

53 →

28 →

20 →

69 →

71 →

47 →

14 →

76 →

11 →

83 →

 **Now try this!**

- **Split the numbers into hundreds, tens and units.**

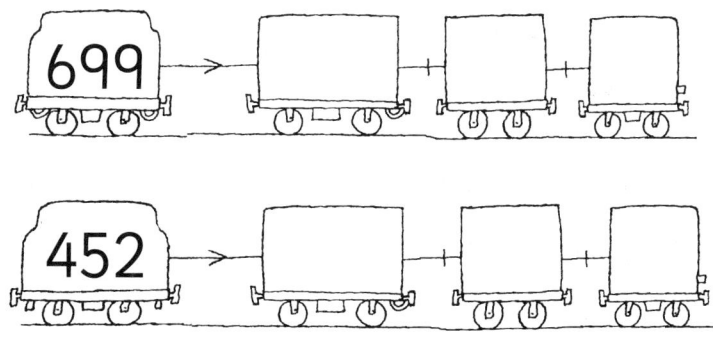

699 →

452 →

Teachers' note Provide place value cards to help the children with this activity.

Developing Numeracy
Numbers and the Number System
Year 3
© A & C Black

Fruity numbers

- **Join the numbers on the fruits to the correct number values.**

4   3   400   2
300   (342)   40

20   9   1   90
10   2   (921)   900

2   20   200   100
1   (214)   10   4

8   700   80   60
6   7   (786)   800   600

500   900
5   (559)   9
90   50

40   400   7
60   (467)   70   600

- **Write five** │three-digit numbers│ **and split them.**

    Example: 345 = 300 + 40 + 5

- **Split five** │four-digit numbers│ **in a similar way.**

Teachers' note Show the children some of these numbers using place value cards to emphasise the value of each digit. Before they complete the the extension activity, ensure that they understand the definition of a three- and four-digit number.

Developing Numeracy
Numbers and the Number System
Year 3
© A & C Black

More splitting numbers

• **Split the numbers into hundreds, tens and units.**

Use place value cards to help you.

Example: 172 = 100 + 70 + 2

246 = ☐ + ☐ + ☐   453 = ☐ + ☐ + ☐

872 = ☐ + ☐ + ☐   921 = ☐ + ☐ + ☐

717 = ☐ + ☐ + ☐   849 = ☐ + ☐ + ☐

531 = ☐ + ☐ + ☐   374 = ☐ + ☐ + ☐

499 = ☐ + ☐ + ☐   605 = ☐ + ☐ + ☐

178 = ☐ + ☐ + ☐   933 = ☐ + ☐ + ☐

Now try this!

• **How many £1 , 10p and 1p coins would you use to make £3.75 and £6.23?**

£3.75 = ____ £1 coins   £6.23 = ____ £1 coins

____ 10p coins   ____ 10p coins

____ 1p coins   ____ 1p coins

Teachers' note In the extension activity, ensure the children hunderstand that they should list how many of each coin they would use to make up the amounts of money. As a further extension, ask the children to partition numbers beyond 1000.

Developing Numeracy
Numbers and the Number System
Year 3
© A & C Black

29

Think of a number

- **Cut out the cards and put them face down.**
- **With a partner, take it in turns to pick a card.**
- **Say a number that fits the rule.**

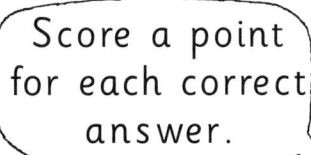

Score a point for each correct answer.

An even number between 50 and 80	A number greater than 700
A number less than 20	The largest two-digit odd number
A number between 70 and 100	The number half-way between 60 and 70
The number half-way between 80 and 100	The sixth number in this pattern: 10, 20, 30, 40…
The largest number less than 600	An odd number greater than 16
A number greater than 100	The smallest odd number
An even number greater than 99	A number between 57 and 67

Now try this!

- **With a partner, make seven more cards.**
- **Use them to play the game again.**

Teachers' note These cards can also be used in the introductory or plenary parts of a lesson with the whole class. The children can use a 100-square to check each other's answers.

Developing Numeracy
Numbers and the Number System
Year 3
© A & C Black

Greater than or less than

- **Cut out the cards and put them face down.**
- **Turn over a card at the same time as your partner.**
- **If your number is greater, say "__ is greater than __",** using the numbers on the cards.
- **Your partner should say "__ is less than __".**
- **How quickly can you describe each pair in this way?**

371	173	237	176
726	723	263	171
333	712	662	232
677	312	727	722
363	111	631	316
271	736	376	166

Teachers' note Speed is encouraged in this game as immediacy of visual recognition is an important skill that the children should develop. A second game can be played where players pick two cards and give a number that lies between them.

Developing Numeracy
Numbers and the Number System
Year 3
© A & C Black

Somewhere in between

• **Write a number that lies between each pair of numbers.**

1. 216 <u>371</u> 564   **2.** 241 ___ 376

3. 475 ___ 576   **4.** 672 ___ 814

5. 339 ___ 628   **6.** 124 ___ 372

7. 617 ___ 896   **8.** 516 ___ 612

9. 108 ___ 180   **10.** 447 ___ 452

Look carefully. The larger number comes first now.

1. 641 ___ 529   **2.** 624 ___ 418

3. 549 ___ 492   **4.** 493 ___ 392

5. 713 ___ 549   **6.** 469 ___ 271

7. 526 ___ 398   **8.** 357 ___ 183

9. 324 ___ 276   **10.** 798 ___ 562

Now try this!

• **Write these numbers in order. Start with the smallest.**

477, 352, 124, 516, 819, 417, 254, 394, 296, 542, 673, 824

_____

_____

Teachers' note As a further extension activity, ask the children to write all the numbers between 396 and 411.

Developing Numeracy
Numbers and the Number System
Year 3
© A & C Black

Follow the paths

- Follow the paths. Add $\boxed{100}$, $\boxed{10}$ or $\boxed{1}$ each time.

17   +100 117 +10 27 +1 18

92   +100 +10 +1

65   +100 +10 +1

26   +100 +10 +1

83   +100 +10 +1

49   +100 +10 +1

94   +100 +10 +1

76   +100 +10 +1

31   +100 +10 +1

Now try this!

57   +500 +20 +3

28   +600 +40 +8

90   +400 +50 +9

Teachers' note The numbers on this sheet could be masked before photocopying for a more flexible resource.

Developing Numeracy
Numbers and the Number System
Year 3
© A & C Black

33

Golf balls

These golf balls are 1, 10, or 100 more or less than the number on the flag. **356**

(357)	(366)	(456)	(355)	(346)	(256)
1 more	10 more	100 more	1 less	10 less	100 less

• Colour the golf balls that are 1, 10, or 100 more or less than the numbers on these flags.

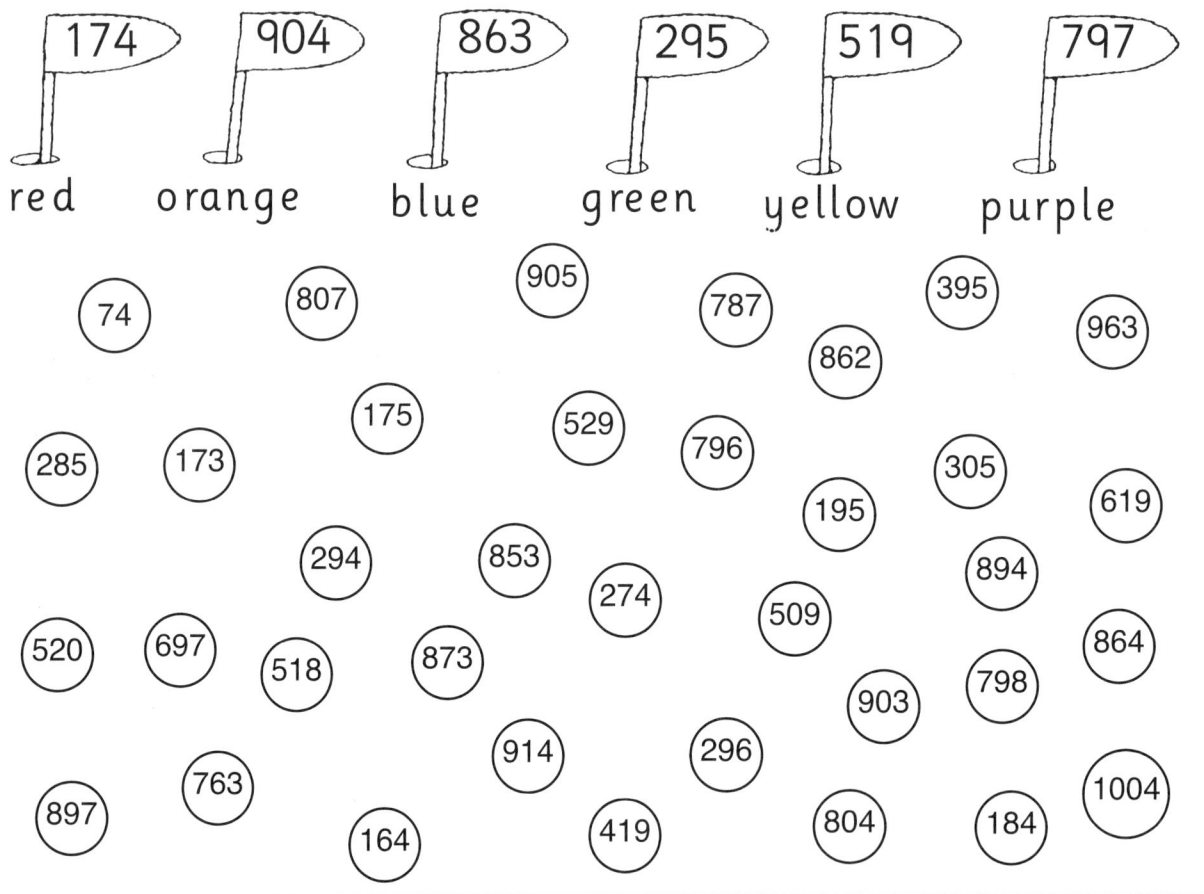

174 — red   904 — orange   863 — blue   295 — green   519 — yellow   797 — purple

74   807   905   787   395   963

285   173   175   529   862   305   619

294   853   796   894   864

520   697   518   873   274   195   798

914   296   509   903   1004

897   763   164   419   804   184

 • Write the numbers on the golf balls for this flag.

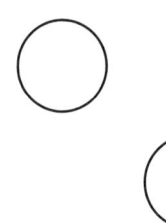 178

Developing Numeracy
Numbers and the Number System
Year 3
© A & C Black

Teachers' note For the main activity, make sure that the children use a different colour for each flag. Remind the children that each ball should be coloured in and each flag should have six corresponding balls.

Order, order!

- **Write the numbers in order. Start with the largest.**

87   64

39   ~~87~~   53   ~~64~~   25

53   72   96   45   14   29   82

34   81   49   73   13   97   52

- **Write the numbers in order. Start with the smallest.**

27   54   38   91   9   63   79

61   60   57   51   49   66   71   69

Now try this!

- **Use the digits** $\boxed{1}$, $\boxed{3}$, $\boxed{5}$ **and** $\boxed{7}$ **to make eight different** $\boxed{\text{two-digit numbers}}$.
- **Write the numbers in order. Start with the smallest.**

Teachers' note The children could use a metre stick, a 0-100 number line or a 100-square to help them with ordering. Before they complete the the extension activity, ensure that they understand the definition of a two-digit number.

**Developing Numeracy
Numbers and the Number System
Year 3
© A & C Black**

Which is the cheapest?

- **Write the prices in order. Start with the lowest.**

66p 52p 79p 80p 19p

19p

_____ _____ _____ _____ _____

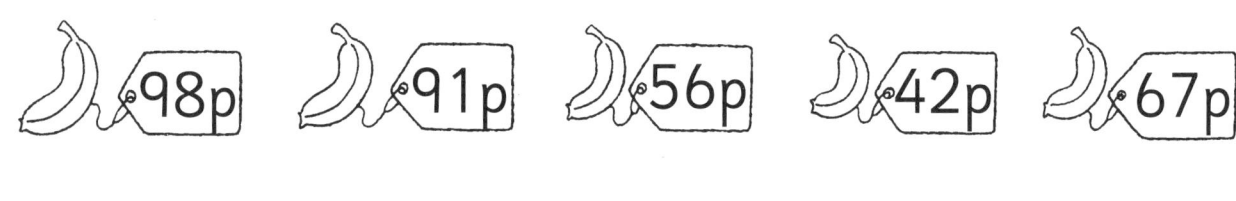

98p 91p 56p 42p 67p

_____ _____ _____ _____ _____

77p 67p 66p 76p 71p

_____ _____ _____ _____ _____

91p 99p 89p 90p 101p

_____ _____ _____ _____ _____

Now try this!

These cakes all cost less than £2.
- **Give each cake a different price.**
- **Write the prices in order. Start with the lowest.**

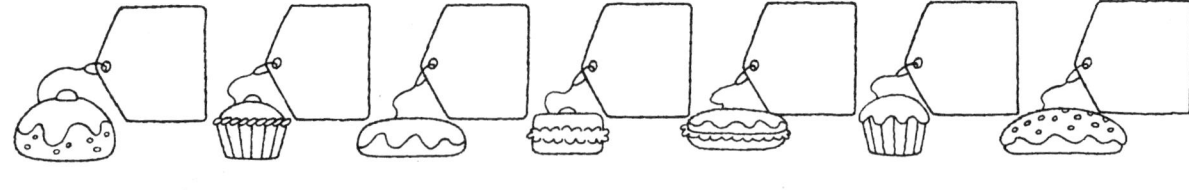

_____ _____ _____ _____ _____ _____ _____

Teachers' note Children can use a metre stick, a 0-100 line or a 100-square to help them with this activity. They might find 0-9 cards useful when creating their own prices in the extension activity.

Developing Numeracy
Numbers and the Number System
Year 3
© A & C Black

Number machines

• Write the numbers in order. Start with the smallest.

819 863
872   798
    891

798

479
507   512
   470
490   497

321
398
312   412
427   418

681   638
712   618
   721
   596

Now try this!

• **How many different** three-digit numbers **can you make from** ③, ⑤, ⑥, ⑦ **and** ⑧ **?**
• **Write them in order. Start with the smallest.**

Teachers' note Provide appropriately labelled number lines (for example, from 790-900) for children who need help with this activity.

Developing Numeracy
Numbers and the Number System
Year 3
© A & C Black

Fairground fun

• **Write the missing numbers.**

347 348 ___ ___ ___ 353

597 ___ ___ 602 ___ ___ ___ 607

• **Write a number in each car so that the numbers are in order.**

450 ___ ___ ___ 611 ___ 620 ___

___ 192 ___ ___ ___ 206 ___ ___ 299 ___

___ ___ ___ 777 ___ ___ 787 ___ ___

991 ___ ___ 998 ___ ___ ___ 1100

Now try this!

1190 ___ ___ ___ 1340

Teachers' note For the second activity, ensure that the children understand that they can write any number lying between two others and that the numbers need not make a constant pattern or sequence.

Developing Numeracy
Numbers and the Number System
Year 3
© A & C Black

Estimate how many

- Estimate how many animals are in each set.
- Count them to see how close you were.

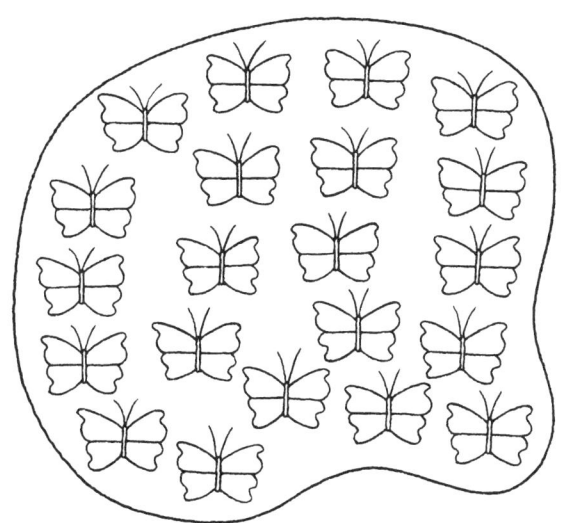

estimate ☐
count ☐

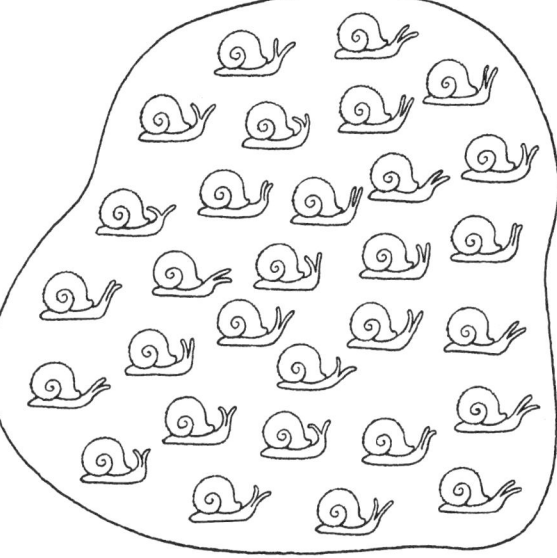

estimate ☐
count ☐

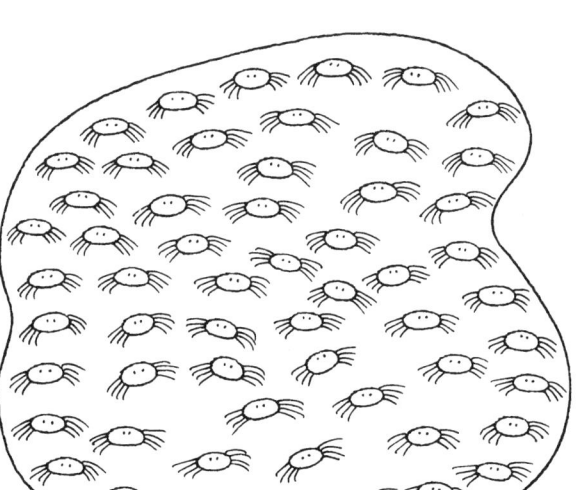

estimate ☐
count ☐

estimate ☐
count ☐

Now try this!

- With a partner, collect a handful of cubes.
- Both of you estimate the number of cubes.
- Count to see whose estimate is closer.

Teachers' note Encourage the children to count a small proportion of the total number to help their estimate. For example, if five represents one quarter, there must be about 20 all together. Remind the children to circle groups of ten as a means of checking their estimates.

Developing Numeracy
Numbers and the Number System
Year 3
© A & C Black

How many sweets?

A jar holds 100 sweets.

- Estimate how many sweets are in each jar.
- Mark the number on the number line.

Don't try to count the sweets.

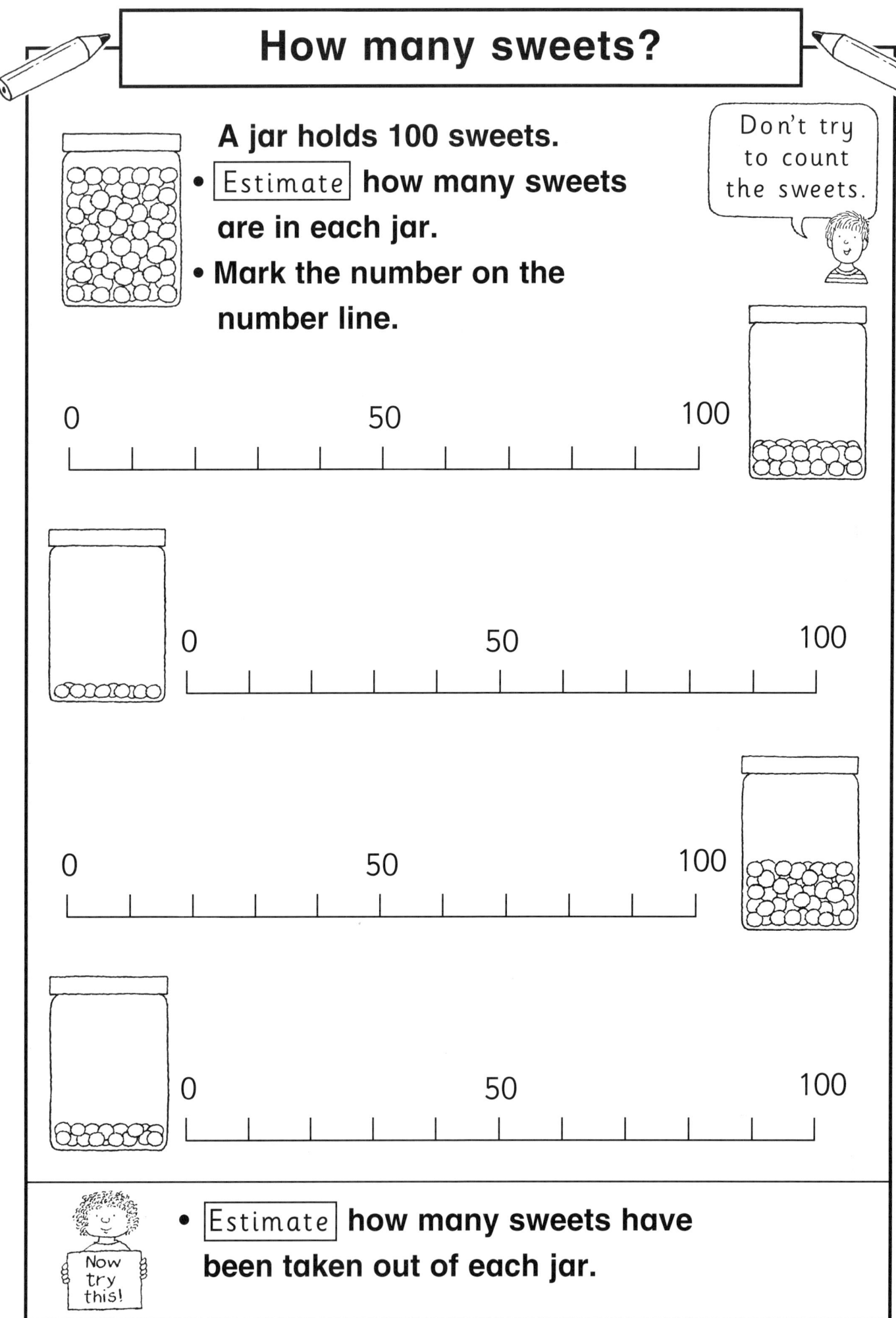

- Estimate how many sweets have been taken out of each jar.

Teachers' note Encourage the children to look at the proportion of each jar which is filled and then to consider this as a fraction of 100 to help their estimates.

Developing Numeracy
Numbers and the Number System
Year 3
© A & C Black

Star numbers

- Estimate the numbers marked by the arrows.

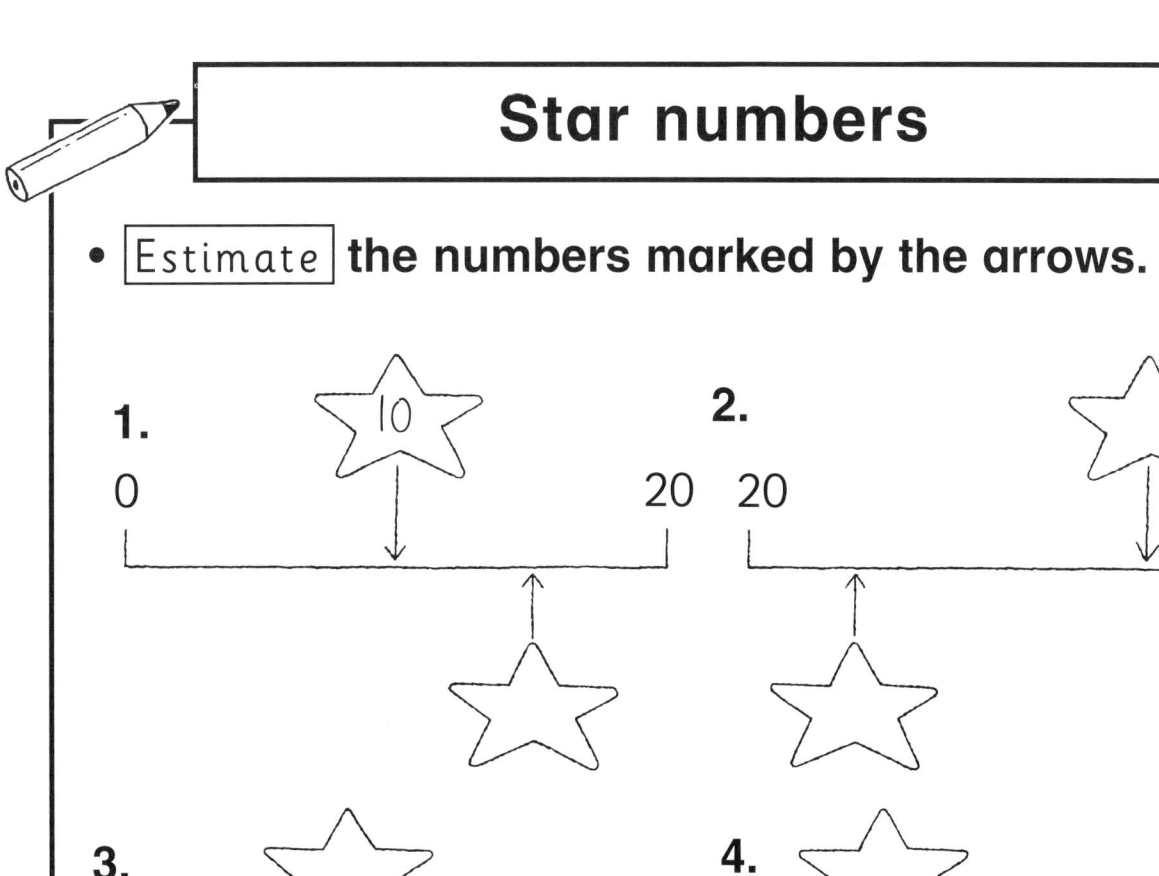

1.
0   20

2.
20   40

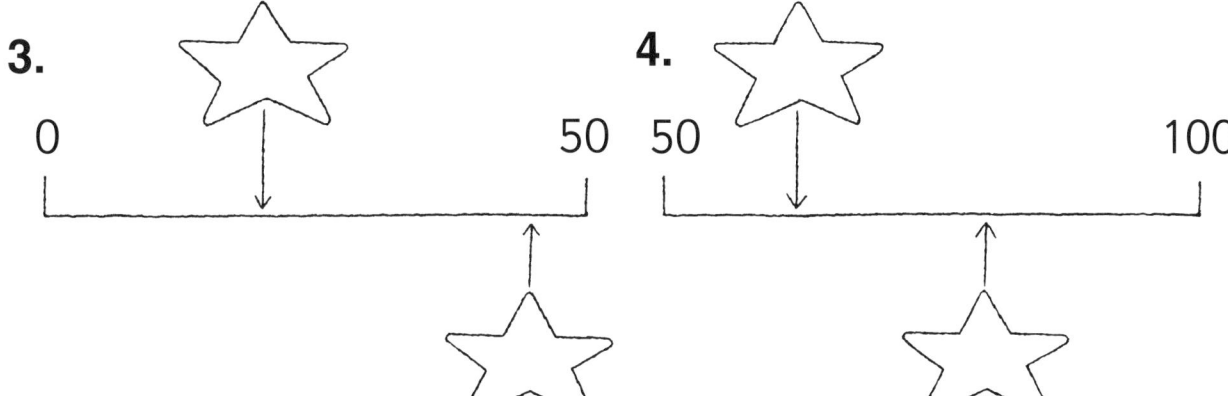

3.
0   50

4.
50   100

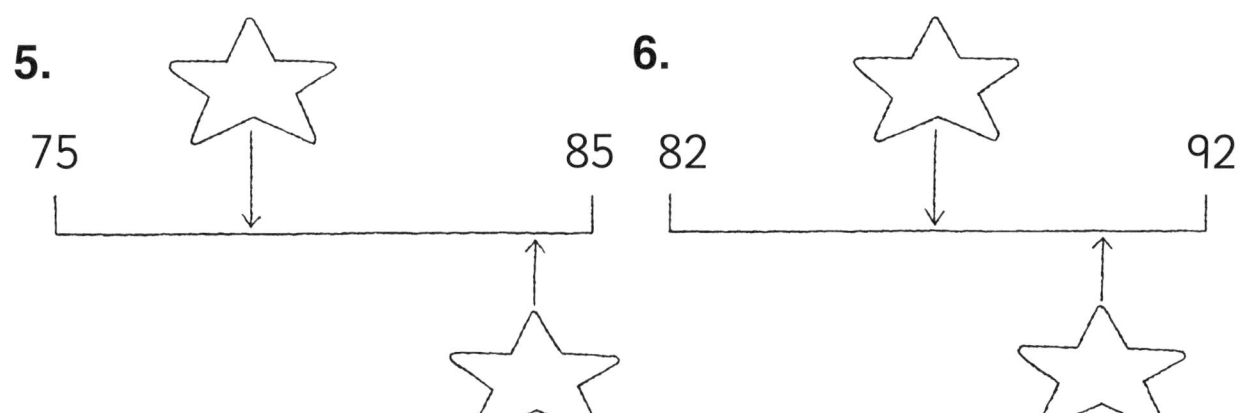

5.
75   85

6.
82   92

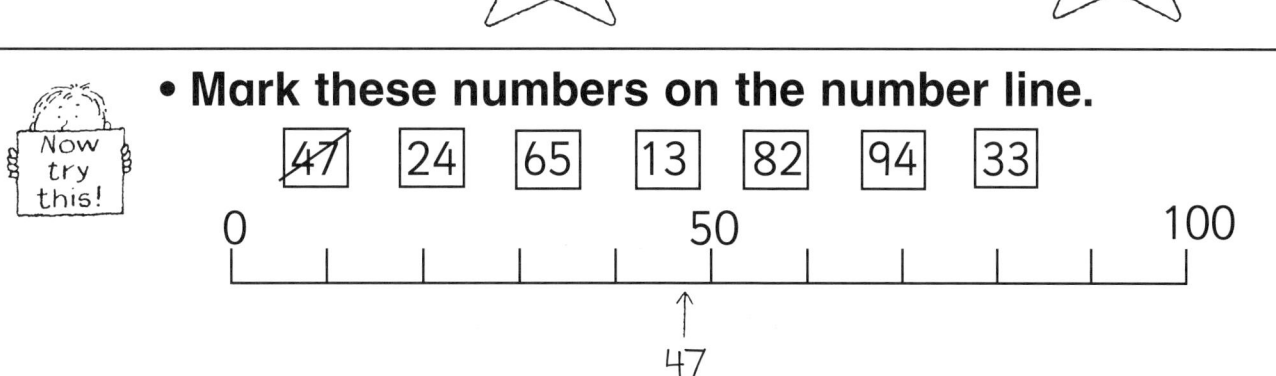

- **Mark these numbers on the number line.**

Now try this!

$\boxed{47}$ $\boxed{24}$ $\boxed{65}$ $\boxed{13}$ $\boxed{82}$ $\boxed{94}$ $\boxed{33}$

0   50   100

47

Teachers' note Provide 0-100 number lines to help the children with this activity.

Developing Numeracy
Numbers and the Number System
Year 3
© A & C Black

Swamp game

- **Take turns to roll a dice and move forward.**
- **When you land on a number ending in five, move on to the nearest** safe **square.**
- **When you roll a six, both players must move on or back to the nearest** safe **square.**

safe										safe	
start **0**	1	2	3	4	5	6	7	8	9	**10**	11

		safe									
											12
22	21	**20**	19	18	17	16	15	14	13		

| 23 | | | | | | | | | | | |

						safe					
24	25	26	27	28	29	**30**	31	32	33		

| | | | | | | | | | | | 34 |

				safe							
44	43	42	41	**40**	39	38	37	36	35		

| 45 | | | | | | | | | | | |

				safe							
46	47	48	49	**50**	51	52	53	54	55		

| | | | | | | | | | | | 56 |

							safe				
67	66	65	64	63	62	61	**60**	59	58	57	

| 68 | | | | | | | | | | | |

	safe									safe	
69	**70**	71	72	73	74	75	76	77	78	79	**80**	81	82

| | | | | | | | | | | | 83 |

					safe						
96	95	94	93	92	91	**90**	89	88	87	86	85	84

		safe								
97	98	99	**100**	finish	

The winner is the first to reach 100!

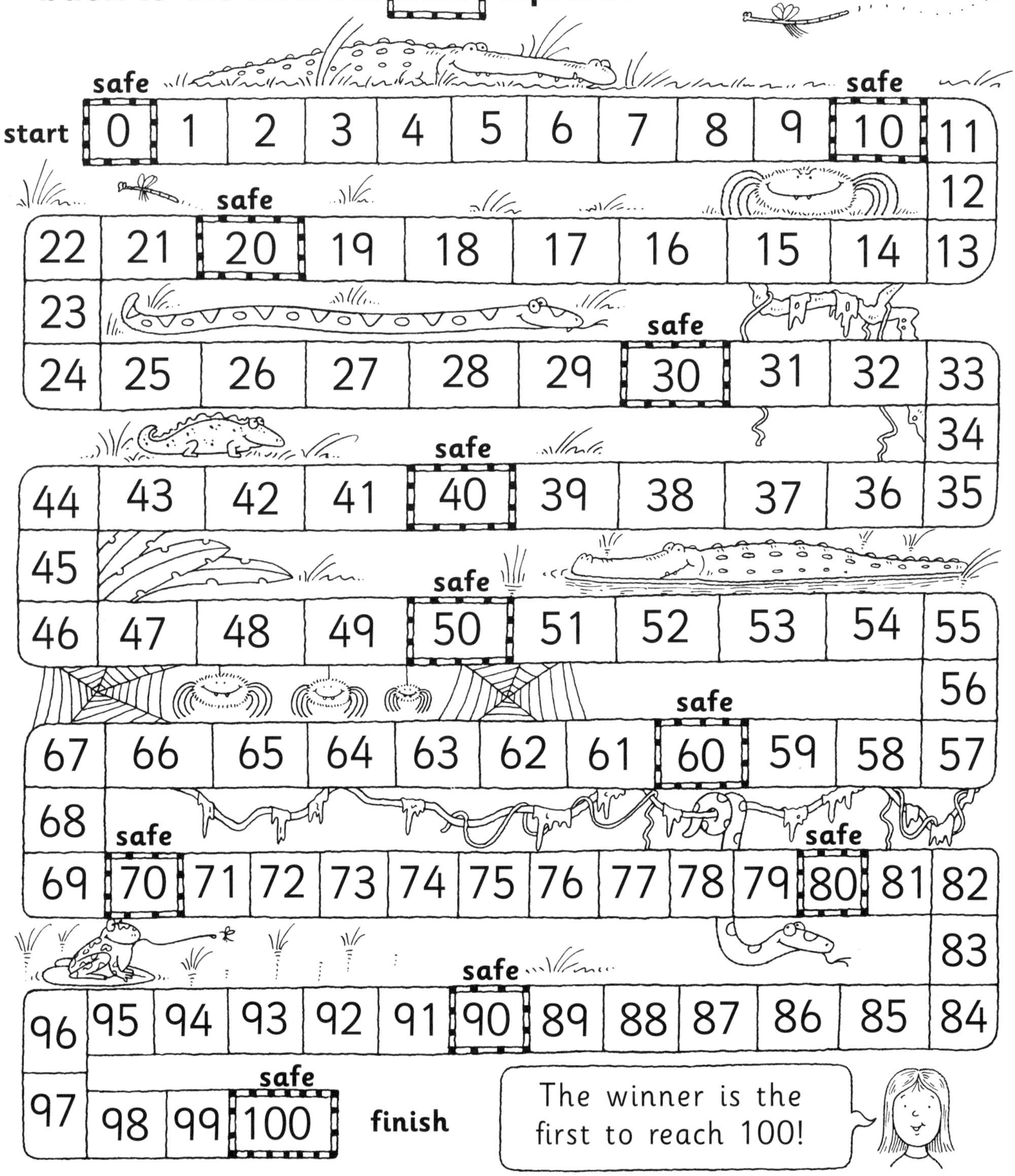

Teachers' note Photocopy this page on to A3 paper or card. The children should play the game in pairs. They will need a counter each and a dice.

Developing Numeracy
Numbers and the Number System
Year 3
© A & C Black

Find the right balance

• Fill in the missing tens.

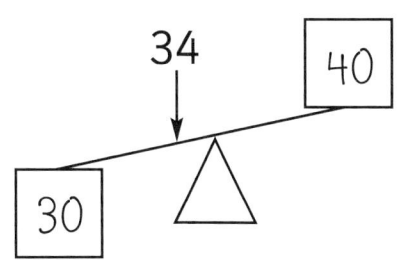

34 → 40
30

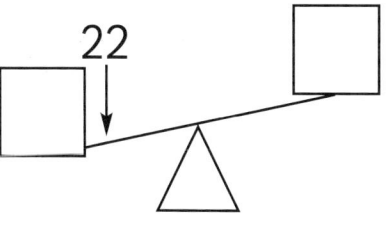

22

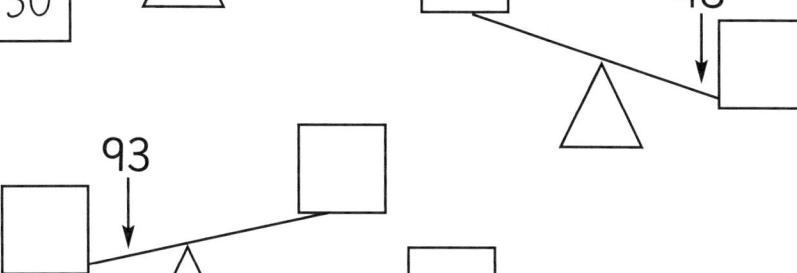

48

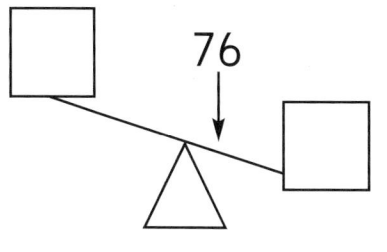

76

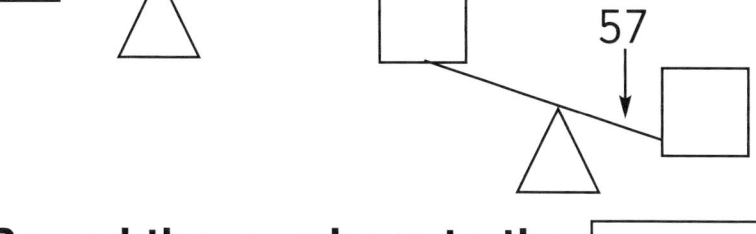

93

57

4

• Round the numbers to the nearest ten **.**

37 → 40   19 → ☐   46 → ☐

23 → ☐   62 → ☐   91 → ☐

55 → ☐   88 → ☐   5 → ☐

4 → ☐   97 → ☐   38 → ☐

41 → ☐   26 → ☐   67 → ☐

Now try this!

• Roll two dice to make a two-digit number **.**

• Write the number rounded to the nearest ten **.**

• Do this ten times.

Example: 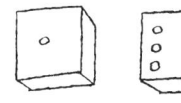  → 20

1   6

Teachers' note Remind the children that if a number has 5 units, they should normally round it up to the next multiple of 10. Draw the children's attention to the number 4 which rounds down to 0.

Developing Numeracy
Numbers and the Number System
Year 3
© A & C Black

Numbers in the news

- Round the number in each headline to the nearest 100.
- Join each headline to its correct position on the number line.

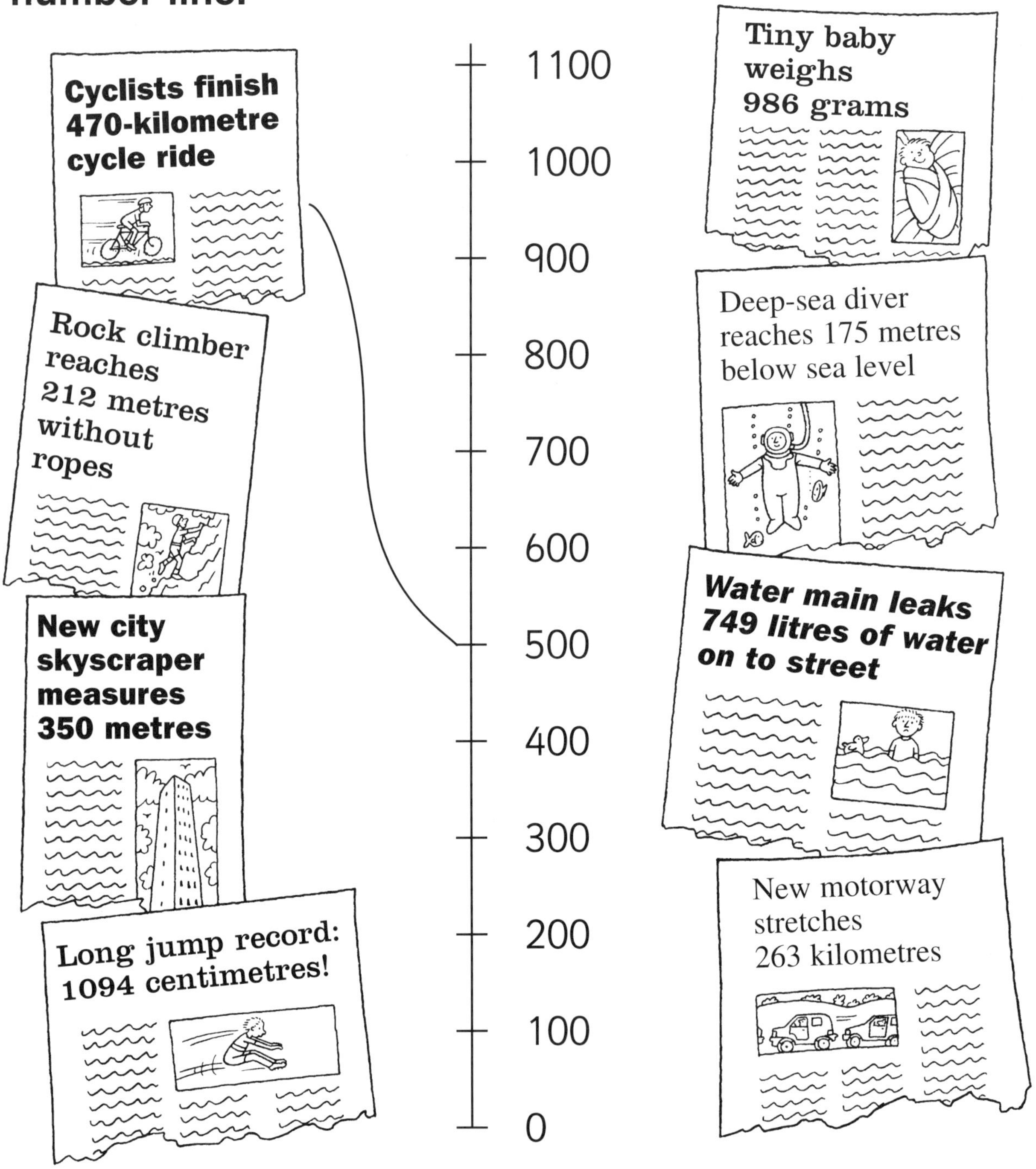

Cyclists finish 470-kilometre cycle ride

Rock climber reaches 212 metres without ropes

New city skyscraper measures 350 metres

Long jump record: 1094 centimetres!

1100

1000

900

800

700

600

500

400

300

200

100

0

Tiny baby weighs 986 grams

Deep-sea diver reaches 175 metres below sea level

Water main leaks 749 litres of water on to street

New motorway stretches 263 kilometres

- **Look in newspapers for six headlines or stories with numbers in them.**
- **Write the numbers rounded to the nearest 100.**

Teachers' note Remind the children that if a number has 5 tens and 0 units, they should normally round up to the next multiple of 100.

Developing Numeracy
Numbers and the Number System
Year 3
© A & C Black

Flower pots

- **Round the numbers to the** `nearest 100`.
- **Use the number line to help you.**

0 100 200 300 400 500 600 700 800 900 1000 1100 1200 1300 1400 1500

175 → 200

970 →

1450 →

230 →

70 →

675 →

1320 →

505 →

615 →

430 →

1110 →

550 →

490 →

370 →

990 →

1275 →

1210 →

780 →

390 →

810 →

225 →

860 →

740 →

915 →

Now try this!

- **Round these numbers to the** `nearest 100`.
- **Which numbers round to 2300?**

| 230 | 2222 | 2345 | 2270 | 2250 |

Teachers' note Remind the children to round to nearest 100 and not to the nearest 10.

Developing Numeracy
Numbers and the Number System
Year 3
© A & C Black

45

Do it yourself

• **Round these measurements to the** nearest 10 cm .

1. 17 cm → 20 cm   **2.** 23 cm →   **3.** 140 cm →

4. 35 cm →   **5.** 44 cm →   **6.** 57 cm →

7. 82 cm →   **8.** 97 cm →   **9.** 85 cm →

• **Round these measurements to the** nearest metre .

1. 1 m 35 cm → 1 m   **2.** 2 m 5 cm →   **3.** 4 m 40 cm →

4. 5 m 15 cm →   **5.** 2 m 25 cm →   **6.** 3 m 75 cm →

7. 9 m 90 cm →   **8.** 7 m 50 cm →   **9.** 6 m 65 cm →

• **Round these measurements to the** nearest 100 m .

1. 97 m → 100 m   **2.** 246 m →   **3.** 567 m →

4. 379 m →   **5.** 450 m →   **6.** 814 m →

7. 175 m →   **8.** 649 m →   **9.** 751 m →

• **Measure the length and width of a table in centimetres. Round each measurement to the** nearest 10 cm **and to the** nearest metre .

Teachers' note Discuss centimetre and metre conversions with the children before they begin this worksheet.

Developing Numeracy
Numbers and the Number System
Year 3
© A & C Black

Odd one out

• **Circle the odd one out in each set.**

1. one half    $\frac{1}{2}$ 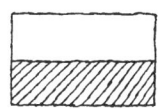   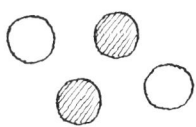

2. 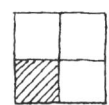   one third   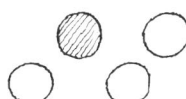   one quarter $\frac{1}{4}$

3. $\frac{3}{4}$ 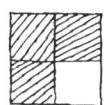   three quarters $\frac{1}{3}$ 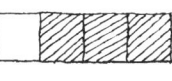

4. $\frac{1}{10}$ one tenth   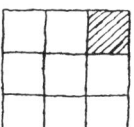   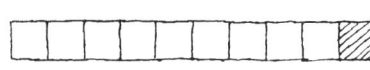

5. one whole   1 $\frac{2}{2}$ 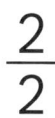 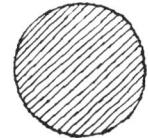   three quarters

6. $\frac{1}{3}$    one third   3   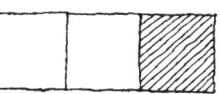

7. two thirds   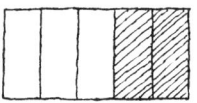 $\frac{2}{3}$    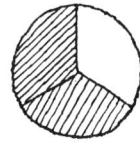

8. 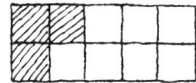 $\frac{3}{10}$ ten thirds   three tenths

Now try this!

• **Draw five more odd one out sets for a friend to try.**

Remember, only one of the fractions should be different in each set.

Teachers' note Each strip could be cut out and used to make an odd one out game.

Developing Numeracy
Numbers and the Number System
Year 3
© A & C Black

47

Fruity fractions

- **What fraction of each set is ringed?**

1.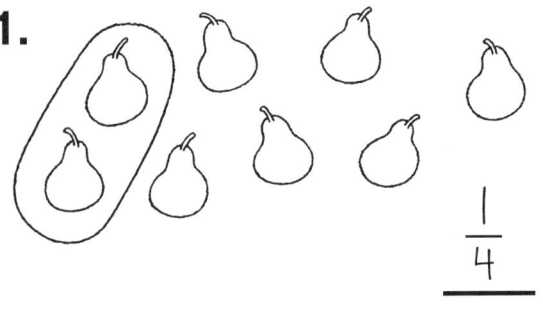

$$\frac{1}{4}$$

2.

___

3.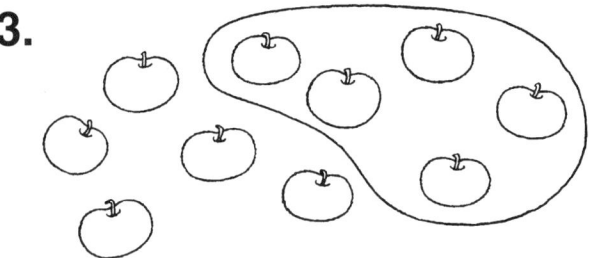

___

4.

___

5.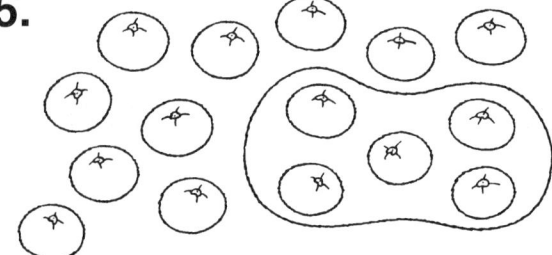

___

6.

___

7.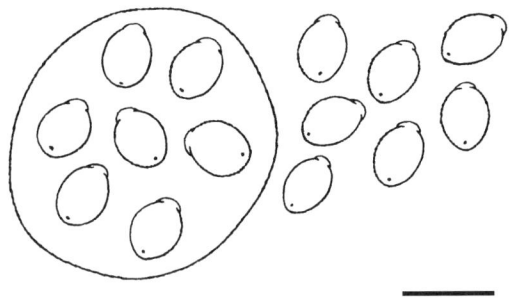

___

8.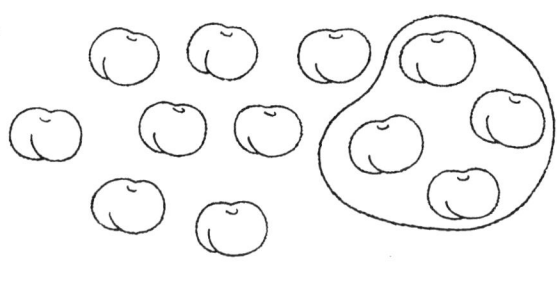

___

Now try this!

- **Collect 24 cubes.**
- **How many is** $\frac{1}{2}$ **of these cubes?** ___
- **How many is** $\frac{1}{4}$ **of these cubes?** ___
- **How many is** $\frac{1}{3}$ **of these cubes?** ___

Teachers' note To extend the main activity, ask the children to find what fraction of each set is not ringed.

Developing Numeracy
Numbers and the Number System
Year 3
© A & C Black

Shady fractions

• **What fraction of each shape is shaded?**

1.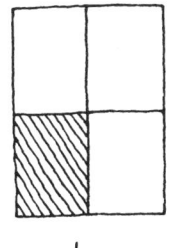

$\dfrac{1}{4}$

2.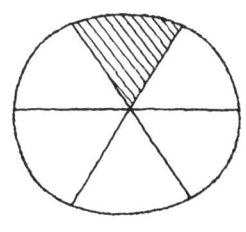

___

3.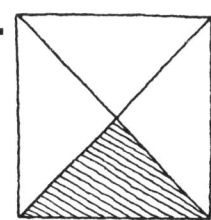

___

4.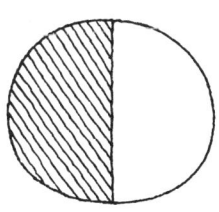

___

5.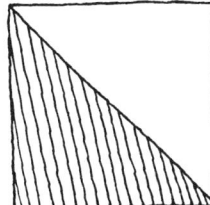

___

6.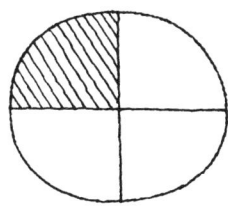

___

7.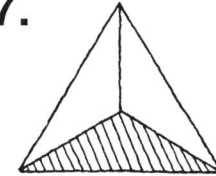

___

8.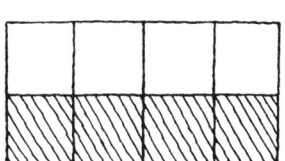

___

• **Colour the correct fractions of these shapes.**

Now try this!

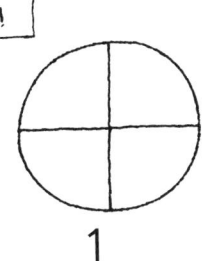

$\dfrac{1}{4}$

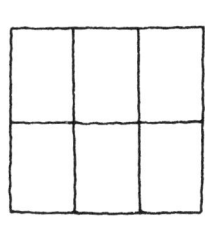

$\dfrac{1}{3}$

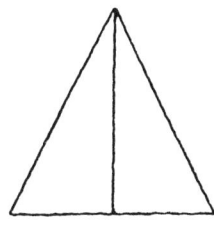

$\dfrac{1}{2}$

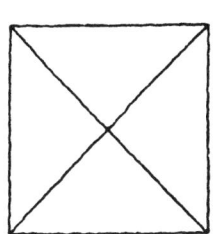

$\dfrac{1}{4}$

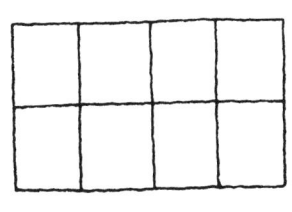

$\dfrac{1}{8}$

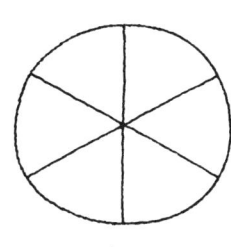

$\dfrac{1}{6}$

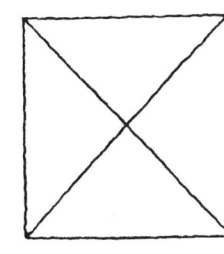

$\dfrac{1}{2}$

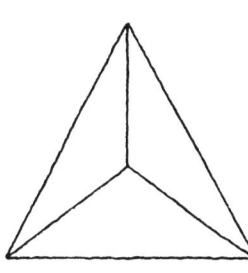

$\dfrac{1}{3}$

Developing Numeracy
Numbers and the Number System
Year 3
© A & C Black

49

Fraction dominoes

- **Play with a friend.**
- **Cut out the dominoes and take five each.**
- **Take turns to try to place a picture domino next to a matching fraction domino.**

	$\dfrac{1}{3}$		$\dfrac{1}{9}$
	$\dfrac{1}{2}$		$\dfrac{1}{10}$
	$\dfrac{1}{5}$		$\dfrac{1}{6}$
	$\dfrac{1}{4}$		$\dfrac{1}{7}$
	$\dfrac{1}{8}$		$\dfrac{1}{12}$

- **Make six different fraction dominoes.**
  Draw a matching picture for each fraction.
- **Use them to play the game.**

Now try this!

Teachers' note Ensure that the children know how to play dominoes before they begin this activity. Encourage them to count the regions of each shape. To understand unit fractions, the children need to appreciate that the number of equal pieces into which the whole is split is the same as the number on the bottom of the fraction.

Developing Numeracy
Numbers and the Number System
Year 3
© A & C Black

Let's divide them up

- **Work out how much each fraction is worth.**

$\frac{1}{5}$ of 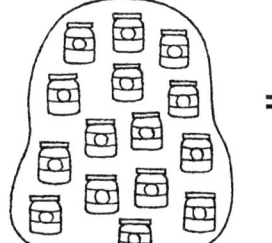 = $\frac{3}{\text{jars of jam}}$

$\frac{1}{8}$ of 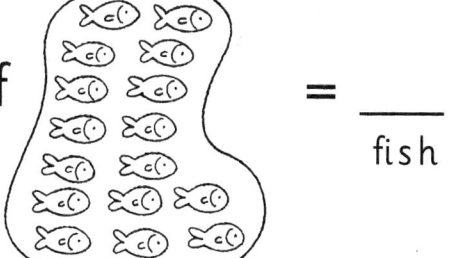 = $\frac{}{\text{fish}}$

$\frac{1}{10}$ of  = $\frac{}{\substack{\text{cans} \\ \text{of beans}}}$

$\frac{1}{6}$ of 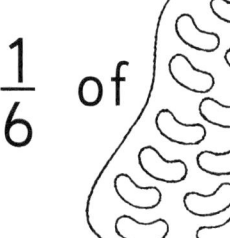 = $\frac{}{\substack{\text{jelly} \\ \text{beans}}}$

$\frac{1}{8}$ of 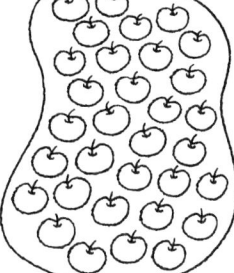 = $\frac{}{\text{apples}}$

$\frac{1}{5}$ of 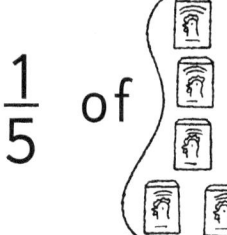 = $\frac{}{\substack{\text{boxes} \\ \text{of cereal}}}$

$\frac{1}{2}$ of 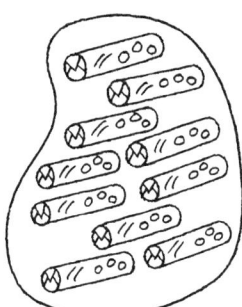 = $\frac{}{\substack{\text{packets} \\ \text{of biscuits}}}$

$\frac{1}{6}$ of 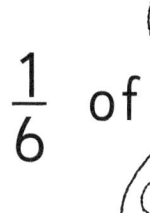 = $\frac{}{\text{eggs}}$

Now try this!

- **Collect 30 cubes.**
- **How many cubes are $\frac{1}{5}$ of the total number?**
- **Now find $\frac{1}{6}$, $\frac{1}{10}$, $\frac{1}{3}$ and $\frac{1}{2}$ of the set of cubes.**
- **Write the numbers.**

Teachers' note If the children need additional help with this activity they could use cubes to replicate each set.

Developing Numeracy
Numbers and the Number System
Year 3
© A & C Black

51

Fraction art

• What fraction of each picture is patterned?

1. $\frac{6}{10}$

2. _____

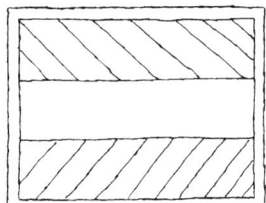

3. _____

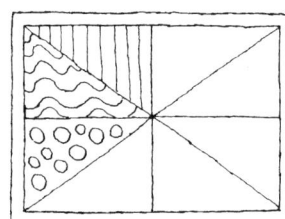

4. _____

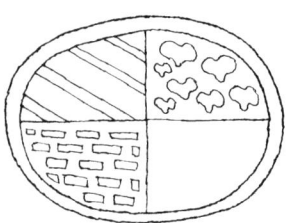

5. _____

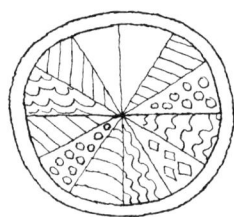

6. _____

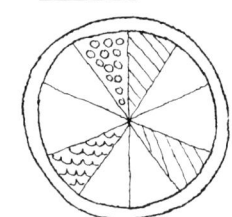

7. _____

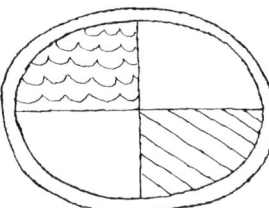

8. _____

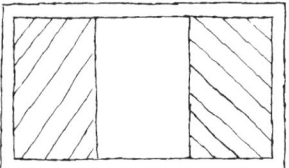

9. _____

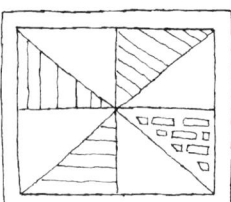

10. _____

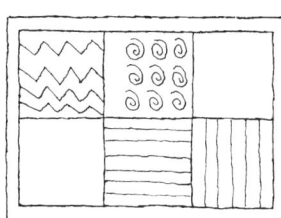

11. _____

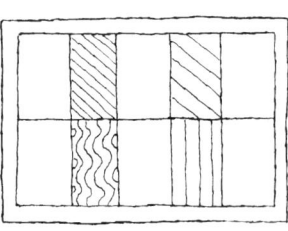

12. _____

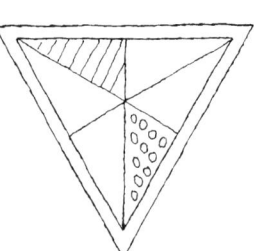

13. _____

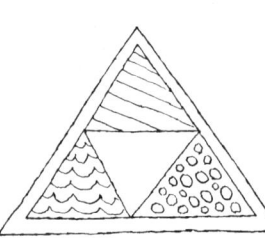

14. _____

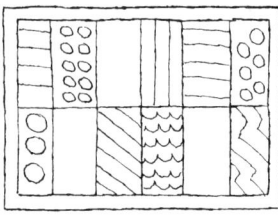

15. _____

Now try this!

• **Draw five more fraction pictures.**

• **Ask a friend to say what fraction is patterned.**

Developing Numeracy
Numbers and the Number System
Year 3
© A & C Black

How many minibeasts?

- **Work out how much each fraction is worth.**
- **Count the sets carefully.**

1.

$\frac{3}{4}$ of 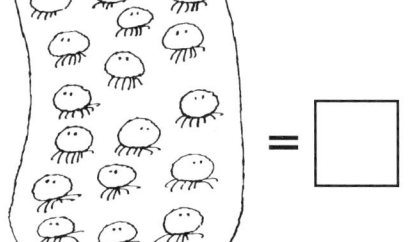 = $\boxed{12}$

2.

$\frac{2}{5}$ of = ☐

3.

$\frac{3}{10}$ of  = ☐

4.

$\frac{4}{7}$ of 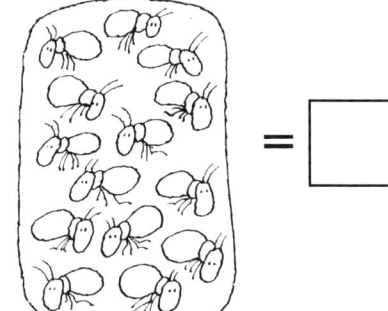 = ☐

5.

$\frac{2}{3}$ of 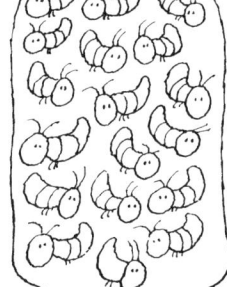 = ☐

6.

$\frac{3}{5}$ of 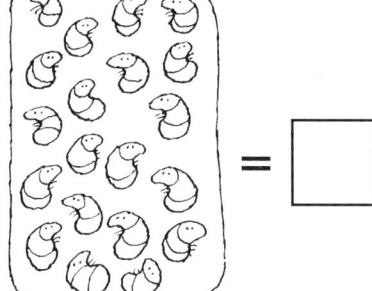 = ☐

7.

$\frac{3}{7}$ of 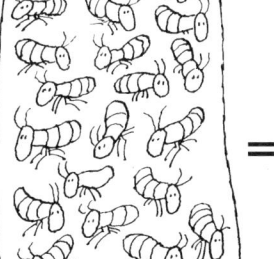  = ☐

8.

$\frac{2}{9}$ of 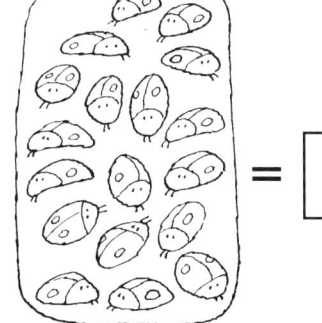 = ☐

- **Collect 24 cubes.**
- **Find** $\boxed{\frac{1}{2}}$, $\boxed{\frac{1}{4}}$, $\boxed{\frac{1}{3}}$, $\boxed{\frac{1}{4}}$ **and** $\boxed{\frac{2}{3}}$ **of the set of cubes.**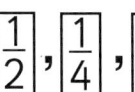

Teachers' note Suggest to the children that they find $\frac{1}{4}$, $\frac{1}{5}$, $\frac{1}{10}$, etc. of each set first to help them complete the main activity. Provide cubes for children to work practically.

Developing Numeracy
Numbers and the Number System
Year 3
© A & C Black

Drawing fractions

- **Colour the correct fraction of each shape on the grid.**

1. Colour $\frac{1}{2}$

2. Colour $\frac{1}{4}$

3. Colour $\frac{3}{4}$

4. Colour $\frac{1}{3}$

5. Colour $\frac{1}{2}$

6. Colour $\frac{3}{10}$

7. Colour $\frac{2}{5}$

8. Colour $\frac{4}{5}$

9. Colour $\frac{3}{4}$

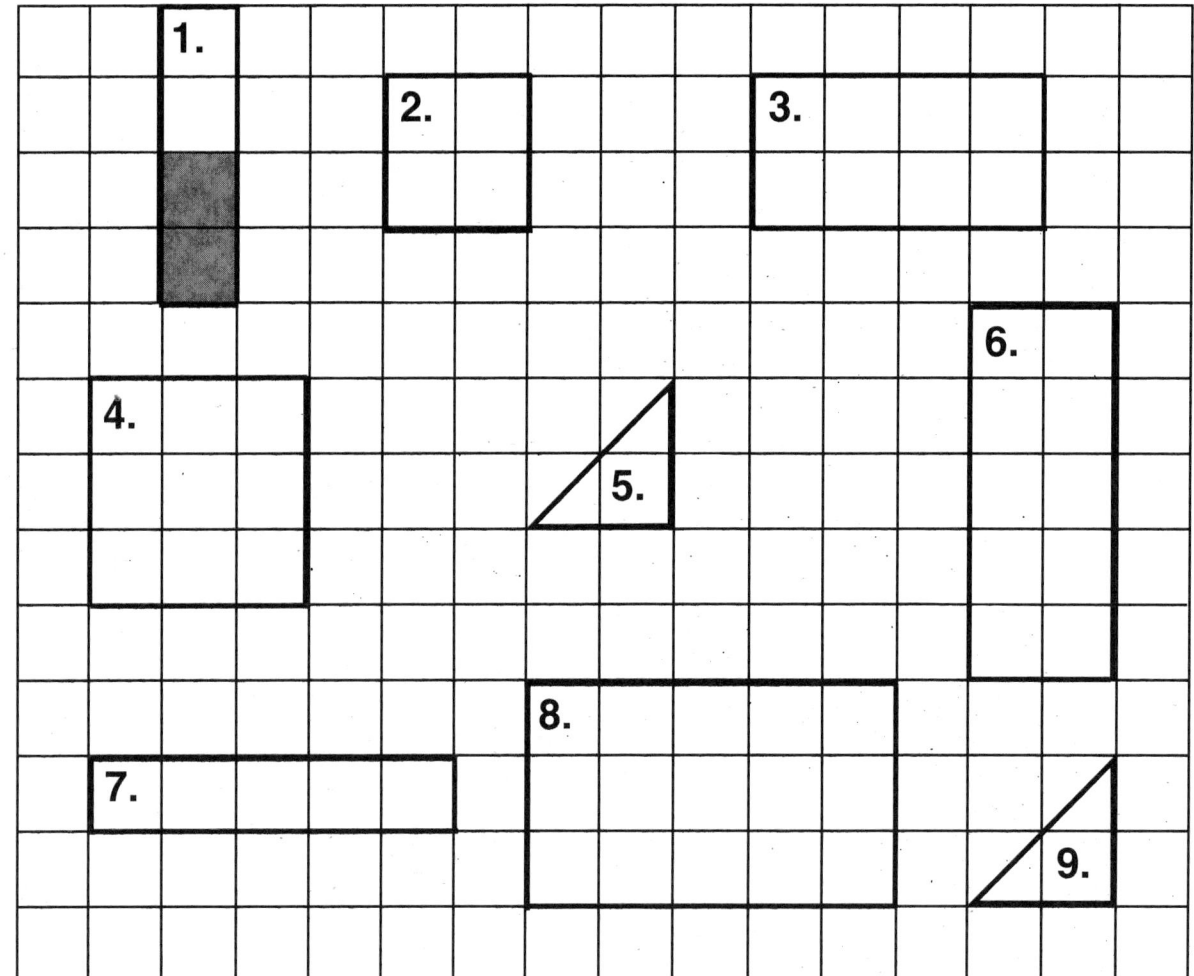

- **What fraction of each shape is not coloured?**

1. _____ **2.** _____ **3.** _____ **4.** _____ **5.** _____

6. _____ **7.** _____ **8.** _____ **9.** _____

Developing Numeracy
Numbers and the Number System
Year 3
© A & C Black

54

A fraction of the price

• **Write the prices on the coins.**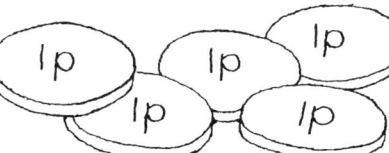

$\frac{1}{2}$ of 10p = 5p $\qquad$ $\frac{1}{3}$ of 9p =

$\frac{1}{5}$ of 15p = $\qquad$ $\frac{1}{4}$ of 16p =

$\frac{1}{10}$ of 30p = $\qquad$ $\frac{1}{8}$ of 24p =

$\frac{1}{3}$ of 15p = $\qquad$ $\frac{1}{5}$ of 20p =

$\frac{1}{2}$ of 18p = $\qquad$ $\frac{1}{4}$ of 12p =

$\frac{1}{8}$ of 16p = $\qquad$ $\frac{1}{10}$ of 20p =

$\frac{1}{3}$ of 18p = $\qquad$ $\frac{1}{4}$ of 24p =

• **Make five more money fraction questions for a friend.**
• **Write down the answers before your friend tries them.**

Teachers' note Provide the children with coins, cubes or counters so that they can work out the answers practically.

Developing Numeracy
Numbers and the Number System
Year 3
© A & C Black

Match patch

• **Draw lines to match the equivalent fractions.**

Use the fraction wall to help you.

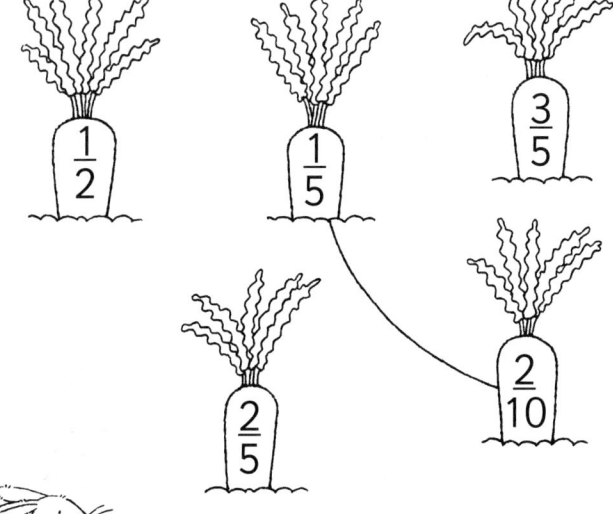

1									
$\frac{1}{2}$					$\frac{1}{2}$				
$\frac{1}{3}$			$\frac{1}{3}$			$\frac{1}{3}$			
$\frac{1}{4}$		$\frac{1}{4}$		$\frac{1}{4}$			$\frac{1}{4}$		
$\frac{1}{5}$		$\frac{1}{5}$		$\frac{1}{5}$		$\frac{1}{5}$		$\frac{1}{5}$	
$\frac{1}{10}$	$\frac{1}{10}$	$\frac{1}{10}$	$\frac{1}{10}$	$\frac{1}{10}$	$\frac{1}{10}$	$\frac{1}{10}$	$\frac{1}{10}$	$\frac{1}{10}$	$\frac{1}{10}$

Now try this!

• **Write five fractions which are equivalent to**

$\frac{1}{2}$ 1 whole

Developing Numeracy
Numbers and the Number System
Year 3
© A & C Black

Teachers' note The children may need help in using the fraction wall to find the equivalent fractions.

Fraction snap

- Cut out the cards.
- Play snap with a friend.
- Call 'snap!' when two fractions are equivalent.

$\dfrac{1}{2}$	$\dfrac{1}{2}$	$\dfrac{1}{2}$	$\dfrac{2}{4}$
$\dfrac{2}{4}$	$\dfrac{5}{10}$	$\dfrac{1}{5}$	$\dfrac{2}{10}$
$\dfrac{2}{5}$	$\dfrac{4}{10}$	$\dfrac{3}{5}$	$\dfrac{6}{10}$
$\dfrac{4}{5}$	$\dfrac{8}{10}$	$\dfrac{2}{2}$	$\dfrac{4}{4}$
$\dfrac{5}{5}$	1	1	$\dfrac{10}{10}$

Developing Numeracy
Numbers and the Number System
Year 3
© A & C Black

Fractions on a pond

- **Write the fractions and whole numbers in order.**
Start with the smallest.

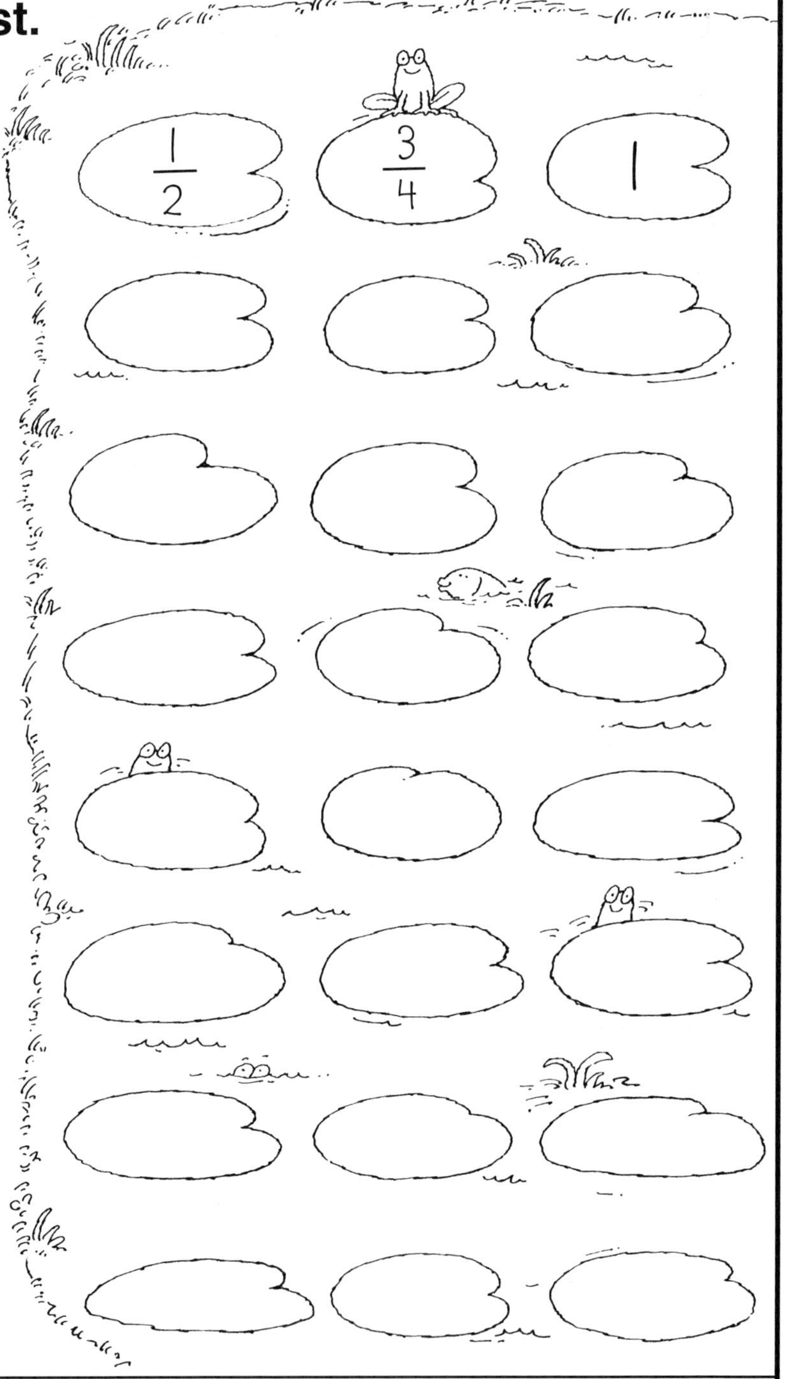

$\frac{3}{4}$ 1 $\frac{1}{2}$

$\frac{1}{2}$ $\frac{1}{4}$ 0

$\frac{1}{2}$ $\frac{3}{4}$ $\frac{1}{4}$

$\frac{5}{10}$ $\frac{1}{4}$ $\frac{3}{4}$

$\frac{3}{4}$ $\frac{1}{4}$ $\frac{2}{4}$

$\frac{7}{10}$ $\frac{3}{5}$ $\frac{1}{5}$

1 $\frac{5}{10}$ $\frac{1}{5}$

$\frac{1}{5}$ $\frac{1}{2}$ 1

Now try this!

$\frac{1}{4}$ $\frac{7}{10}$ $\frac{3}{5}$

$\frac{4}{5}$ $\frac{1}{2}$ $\frac{3}{10}$

Teachers' note Some children may need a fraction wall to help them complete this activity.

Developing Numeracy
Numbers and the Number System
Year 3
© A & C Black

Froggy fractions

- **These frogs jump in** `halves` **.**
  Continue the lines to show where
  the frogs land.

0   1   2   3   4

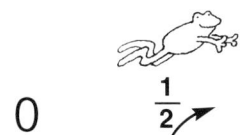

0   $\frac{1}{2}$ 1   2   3   4

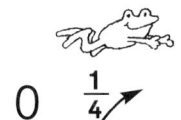

0   $\frac{1}{4}$ 1   2   3   4

- **This frog jumps in** `quarters` **. Continue the line.**

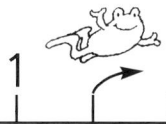

0   1   2   3   4

Now try this!

- **Start from** $2\frac{1}{4}$ **.**
- **Jump in** `quarters` **for three hops.**
- **Where does the frog finish?** _____

0   1   2   3   4

Where does the frog finish if you start from $1\frac{1}{4}$ **?** _____
Where does the frog finish if you start from $\frac{1}{4}$ **?** _____
Where does the frog finish if you start from $3\frac{1}{4}$ **?** _____

Teachers' note You could demonstrate these ideas at the front of the class by inviting a child to hop along a number line. Encourage the children to say the numbers aloud to emphasise the patterns.

Developing Numeracy
Numbers and the Number System
Year 3
© A & C Black

Fraction name game

- **Roll the dice and move forward.**
- **If you get a question wrong, go back three spaces.**

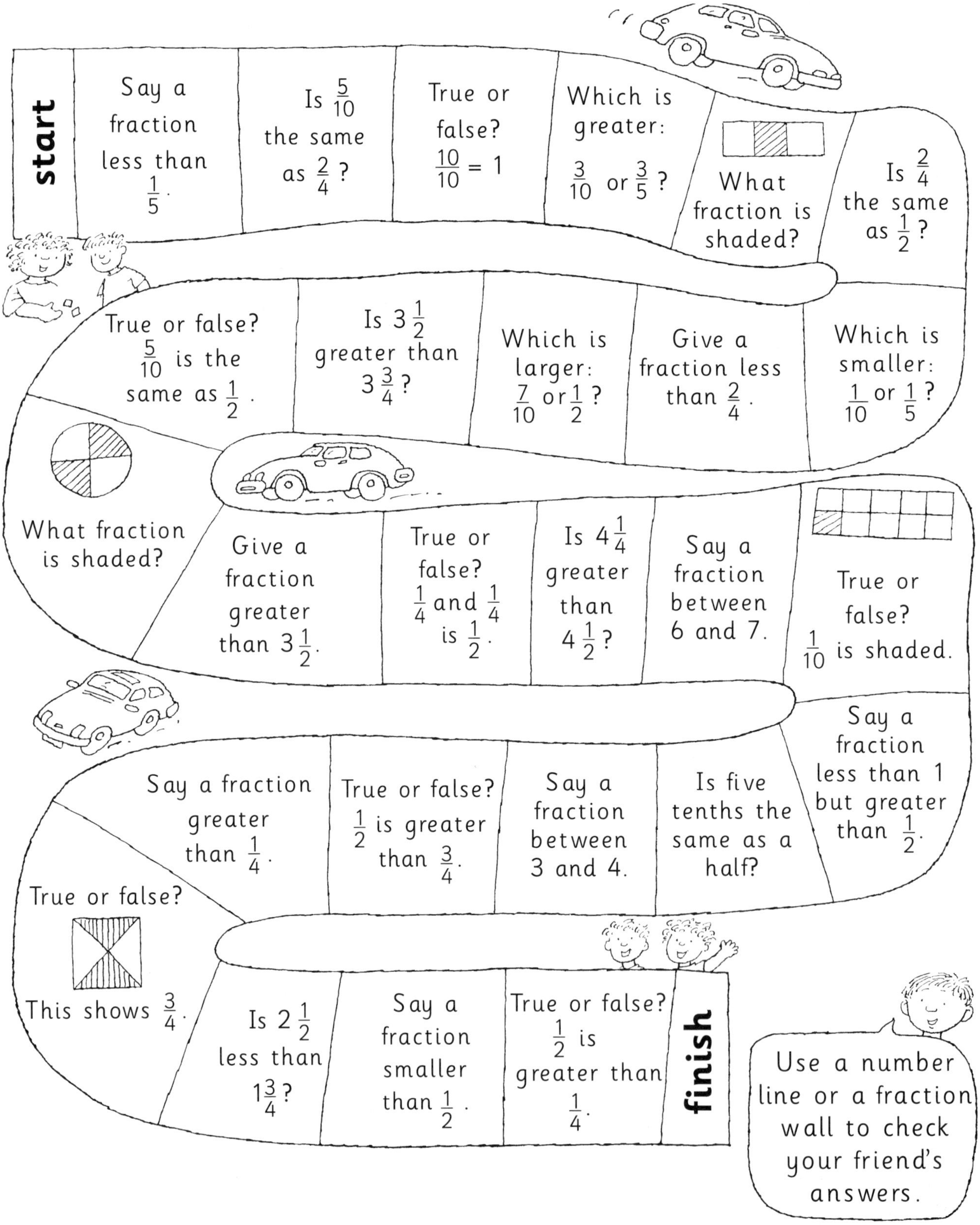

start

Say a fraction less than $\frac{1}{5}$.

Is $\frac{5}{10}$ the same as $\frac{2}{4}$?

True or false? $\frac{10}{10} = 1$

Which is greater: $\frac{3}{10}$ or $\frac{3}{5}$?

What fraction is shaded?

Is $\frac{2}{4}$ the same as $\frac{1}{2}$?

True or false? $\frac{5}{10}$ is the same as $\frac{1}{2}$.

Is $3\frac{1}{2}$ greater than $3\frac{3}{4}$?

Which is larger: $\frac{7}{10}$ or $\frac{1}{2}$?

Give a fraction less than $\frac{2}{4}$.

Which is smaller: $\frac{1}{10}$ or $\frac{1}{5}$?

What fraction is shaded?

Give a fraction greater than $3\frac{1}{2}$.

True or false? $\frac{1}{4}$ and $\frac{1}{4}$ is $\frac{1}{2}$.

Is $4\frac{1}{4}$ greater than $4\frac{1}{2}$?

Say a fraction between 6 and 7.

True or false? $\frac{1}{10}$ is shaded.

Say a fraction less than 1 but greater than $\frac{1}{2}$.

Say a fraction greater than $\frac{1}{4}$.

True or false? $\frac{1}{2}$ is greater than $\frac{3}{4}$?

Say a fraction between 3 and 4.

Is five tenths the same as a half?

True or false? This shows $\frac{3}{4}$.

Is $2\frac{1}{2}$ less than $1\frac{3}{4}$?

Say a fraction smaller than $\frac{1}{2}$.

True or false? $\frac{1}{2}$ is greater than $\frac{1}{4}$.

finish

Use a number line or a fraction wall to check your friend's answers.

Teachers' note Photocopy this page on to A3 paper or card. The children could play this game in pairs. They will need a dice and a counter each.

Developing Numeracy
Numbers and the Number System
Year 3
© A & C Black

A fraction left

- **What fraction of each cake or pizza do you think has been eaten? What fraction is left?**

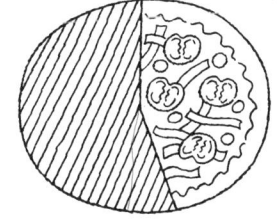

eaten _____ left _____   eaten _____ left _____

eaten _____ left _____   eaten _____ left _____

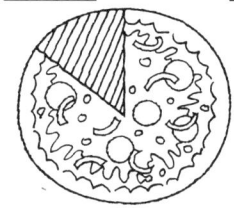

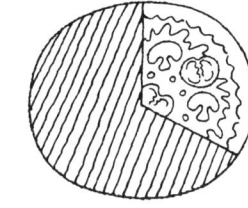

eaten _____ left _____   eaten _____ left _____

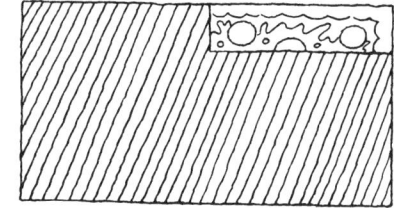

eaten _____ left _____   eaten _____ left _____

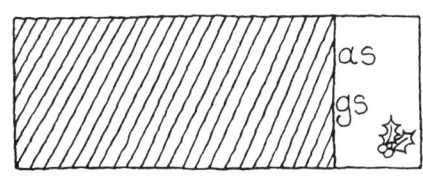

eaten _____ left _____   eaten _____ left _____

- **Draw two more fraction cakes or pizzas.**
- **Ask a friend to write how much has been eaten and how much is left.**

Teachers' note Children are estimating these fractions so encourage them to use the appropriate vocabulary such as 'about' and 'approximately'.

Developing Numeracy
Numbers and the Number System
Year 3
© A & C Black

Time estimates

• **Fill in the missing fractions.**

It is about _____ past three.

It is about _____ to twelve.

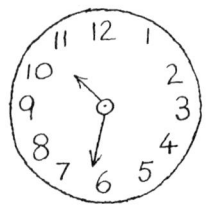

It is about _____ past ten.

It is nearly _____ past one.

It is just after _____ to five.

It is approximately _____ past seven.

• **Write in words the approximate times.**

7:31	_____
11:14	_____
2:46	_____
6:17	_____

Teachers' note Encourage the children to approximate times in this way throughout the school day. They should use a range of vocabulary.

Developing Numeracy
Numbers and the Number System
Year 3
© A & C Black

Dividing lines

Each number line has a number in a circle.

- Draw an arrow to show half of the number in the circle.

1.

2.

3.

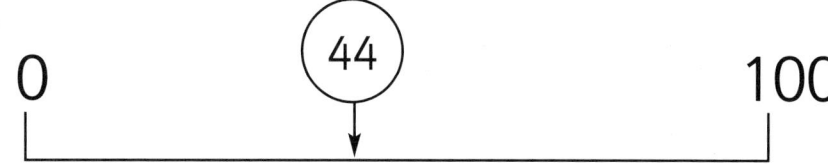

4.

5.

6.

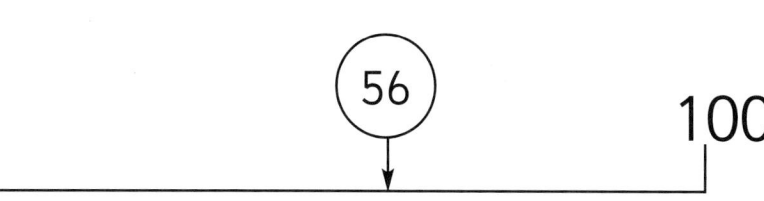

- **Work out what is half of the number in each circle.**

1. _____ 2. _____ 3. _____ 4. _____ 5. _____ 6. _____

Teachers' note Provide number lines with each number marked, or use metre sticks to help the children with this activity.

Developing Numeracy
Numbers and the Number System
Year 3
© A & C Black

Fraction estimates

- Estimate what fraction of each container is filled.

1.

2.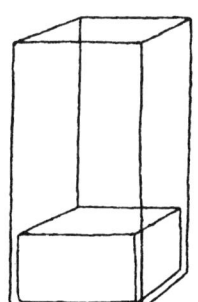

3.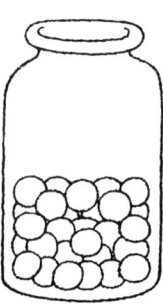

_____

4.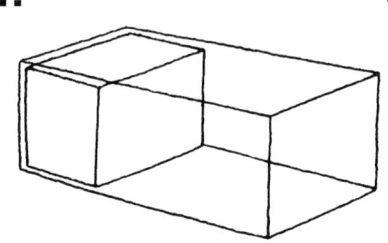

5.

6.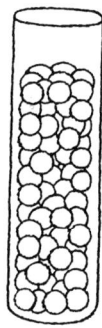

_____

7.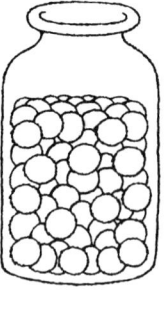

8.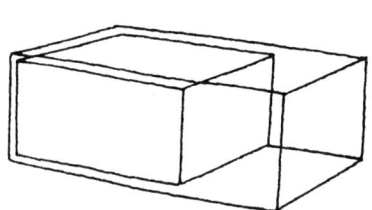

9.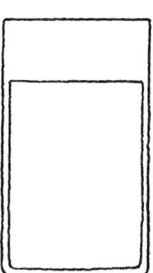

_____

Now try this!

- **What fraction of each container is empty?**

1. _____ 2. _____ 3. _____ 4. _____ 5. _____

6. _____ 7. _____ 8. _____ 9. _____

Teachers' note Before the children attempt this page, they should estimate in practical situations the fraction of a container that is filled/empty.

**Developing Numeracy
Numbers and the Number System
Year 3
© A & C Black**